Golf Magazine's TIPS
from the Teaching Pros

Golf Magazine's

TIPS from the Teaching Pros

by the Editors of *Golf Magazine*

Illustrations by Dom Lupo and Lealand Gustavson

Harper & Row, Publishers

New York, Evanston, and London

LIBRARY OF CONGRESS CATALOG CARD NUMBER: 69–15310

Contents

IV. THE SHORT GAME

V. THE SAND TRAP

VI. PUTTING

Introduction

Over the years, *Golf Magazine* has published a number of instruction books that were designed to help the average golfer improve his game. There have been volumes of *Pro Pointers* as well as books devoted entirely to such things as the long game and the short game—and the response has been such that there can be no doubt they have fulfilled their purpose. Now, encouraged by this response and with confidence born of experience, we have compiled a book that we feel will be even more helpful, a book by the teaching professionals themselves.

A quick survey of the shelves in any bookstore will reveal dozens of books by well-known tournament players, men who sought to cash in quickly before the luster wore off their triumphs. Sometimes these books are quite useful—and a few have been outstanding—but the majority contain little more than a stereotyped rundown of the same material you have read many times before. It was recognition of the fact that there is a lot of instruction available in books, but not much good instruction, that led to this book.

You will recall from your school days that it was the second-string guard sitting on the bench who grew up to be the successful coach, while the star player usually proved to be unsuccessful at teaching others. This analogy applies to golf in full measure. Your local club pro couldn't win the U.S. Open—he probably couldn't even qualify for the tournament—but he can tell you more about your game than 90 percent of the touring pros.

Here, then, is a collection of tips from the teaching pros, the men who make their living helping others play the game better. We don't guarantee you will win the U.S. Open after reading this book, but you should certainly send the members of your weekend foursome reaching for their pocketbooks. And isn't that why most of us keep playing this game?

The Editors

Golf Magazine's TIPS
from the Teaching Pros

I. THE FUNDAMENTALS

Golf, as you figured out long ago, is a difficult game to play really well; but contrary to what you might think, it isn't at all difficult to play reasonably well. In other words, everybody should be able to break a hundred, and all the hundred-shooters should be breaking 90. Certainly, common sense and a little thought *before* making the shot have a lot to do with it, but the man who has mastered the fundamentals can shoot a pretty good game even without common sense.

The trouble with most golfers is that they think they already know the fundamentals, with the result that they pass over such tiresome instruction in search of something more esoteric. Everyone is constantly looking for "The Secret." Well, the secret is in learning the fundamentals, and if you're really honest with yourself, you'll admit that your right hand is a little too far under the shaft, or you tend to jerk the club back instead of sweeping it back smoothly, or that you start the downswing with your hands instead of your hips, or that you've unconsciously fallen into some other bad habit. Take a good, hard look at these basics and see if you don't start playing better.

The Right Swing for You

by Harry Obitz and Dick Farley

The type of swing you should use already has been determined by your physique. In the same way that a tall, slender person takes longer strides than the short, chunky type, so these widely differing builds should employ modifications from the classic swing to get the most out of their physical equipment.

While no two human beings are exactly alike in build, it is possible to draw some useful guidelines. As a general rule of thumb, the taller and more slender you are, the more upright you should swing. The shorter and chunkier you are, the flatter your swing should be to get maximum power.

Let's deal with the tall, slender type first.

The willowy six-footer has one built-in advantage over his shorter golfing brothers in that he will naturally have a longer swing arc. This, in turn, should produce greater clubhead speed and, therefore, greater power. Being slighter all over than the chunky player, he also tends to be more supple. He therefore has little difficulty in taking a full shoulder turn, with his back toward the hole, and a full hip turn, generally about half that of the shoulders. Chunky players must often settle for less than this to avoid pulling their head off the ball to the right on the way back.

A person of tall, slender build should use a slightly narrower stance than normal. He doesn't displace so much weight as a chunky player or have to worry about such a large transfer of weight during the swing. A fairly narrow stance also will help him take the full shoulder and hip turn that produces a long arc.

The slim six-footer will find it easiest to use a "hands-and-arms" swing, so called because these are the parts of the body that you concentrate on "feeling" during the swing. You start the clubhead away from the ball with the left hand and then halfway back (where the shaft becomes horizontal to the ground) both arms swing the club up to the correct top-of-the-swing position. The left arm remains extended and the

2

Tall player, *left,* takes club back with "feel" focused in hands and arms. Short, chunky man, *right,* with "feel" in shoulders. With average build, the "feel" is in a combination of both.

TALL, SLENDER
This player should use slightly narrower stance than normal to get full hip and shoulder turn.

AVERAGE
This player should use normal stance, with feet approximately shoulder-width apart.

SHORT, CHUNKY
This player should use a wider stance than normal to brace against overshifting weight.

3

right arm folds quietly into the right side. The right forearm aids the left arm in keeping the plane of the swing established.

At the top of the swing for the tall, slender player, the club shaft *will lie closer to the base of the neck than the point of the right shoulder.* On the downswing, the action starts with the heel of the left hand and left arm pulling down at the ball. The body will then react to this through the ball into a complete finish.

The key, then, to the slender man's swing is concentrating on the use of the hands and arms, because by this method he will get a wider and higher swing arc. This will compensate for the lack of bulk or sheer muscle he has to put into the shot. It will also prevent excess body motion during the swing and tend to keep the player steady over the ball.

The large swing arc gives the tall player a longer time in the downswing to be in proper position to strike the ball, or to compensate for any slight error he might have made as regards clubface alignment or path of swing. However, he must remember that it takes more time to complete a longer swing. *He must never rush the swing.*

The tall, slender player has longer working parts—arms, legs, etc.—than the person of average build and must give himself time to allow these parts to do their work thoroughly. Tied in with this is the consideration that he must also guard against overswinging, a faulty action that his muscles are not strong enough to control. Tall tournament stars such as Al Geiberger and Bob Charles avoid this mistake by holding their backswing, even on full shots, to a point where the shaft is just about parallel to the ground, but no further.

Another point the tall, slim player should watch is his address position. He must guard against too much forward bend at the waist and "reaching" for the ball. Somehow this seems instinctive for him—perhaps because he is conscious that his height puts him farther away from the ball than shorter golfers, and feels that "getting down to it" will give him more control. This fault, however, makes the plane of his swing too erratic and is a great cause of heeling the ball and slicing, as from this cramped address position he is likely to roll the face of the club open as he goes back.

Dropping the head on the downswing is another fault of the slim six-footer. Because his swing is more nearly vertical (upright) than that of the person of average build, the force of the swinging clubhead tends to

TALL, SLENDER
Using hands-and-arms swing, this player will swing club back in upright plane, *above*. At top, club will be over a line more toward base of neck than point of right shoulder, *below*.

AVERAGE
Using "classic" swing, this player will take club back in medium plane, *above*. At top, club will be over a line about midway between base of neck and point of right shoulder, *below*.

SHORT, CHUNKY
Using shoulder swing, this player will turn first, bringing swing inside on flat plane, *above*. At top, club will be over a line more toward point of right shoulder than base of neck, *below*.

make him collapse his knees on the downswing, his head drops down and he gets a fine assortment of "fat" shots, "scoops," and "pop flies." If this sounds like you, try to keep your head steady throughout the swing.

Tall players should also know how to correct the fault where their ball is pushed to the right with severe loss of power. Usually, this is caused by their sliding their entire body, and most importantly, their head, past the ball before impact. This weakens the hit and opens the clubface at

5

impact, causing a push to the right. Emphasis on keeping the head *back* of the ball on the downswing through impact can help solve this problem.

The strengths and problems of the short, chunky player are, as you would expect, just the reverse of those of the tall, slender man.

The short, chunky player has strong shoulders, arms, legs; in fact, he tends to be strong most everywhere. His great difficulty in making the swing is that he usually lacks suppleness and agility. Because of his heavy build, he cannot make as full a body turn as the slender, tall player without moving his head off the ball or swaying. Therefore, his body turn should be less full than that of the tall, slender player.

Players of stocky build should use a "shoulder" swing. Like the hands-and-arms swing, this swing is so called because the shoulders are the parts of the body concentrated on while executing the swing. The swing starts with a dipping action of the left shoulder under the chin, and a raising and a lateral action of the right shoulder. This turning and tilting action of the shoulders does the majority of the work in carrying the arms, hands and club back to the proper position.

At the top, the chunky person will find his club shaft positioned *more toward the point of the right shoulder than to the base of the neck.* This is what is meant by a flat swing, a result of the body turning first, bringing the swing inside and therefore on a flatter plane.

On the downswing, you concentrate on returning the left shoulder in a circular movement to the same position it had at address. At the top, the left shoulder was under your chin. You now think of the shoulder moving up and to the left. The upper arms are held in close to the body and react to the action of the shoulders. In the hitting area, the chunky player should think of supplying increased power by use of the right forearm. The action is similar to that used in bowling or a forehand stroke in tennis.

One of the problems of the chunky player is that he usually cannot cock his wrists as fully as the tall, slender person. He tends to "hit from the top" and lose the power in his hands and wrists. Concentration on the use of the right forearm on the downswing will help him keep his wrists cocked and give him proper hand action at the ball.

By using the shoulders as the motivating force of the swing, the chunky person is better able to keep his balance, and use his hips, knees and feet properly, without giving direct thought to using them. He

6

eliminates the necessity of studying the component parts of the swing if he just focuses his attention on the action of the shoulders.

The key move that will make or mar the swing of the stocky player is the initial action of the left shoulder. If he concentrates on getting his left shoulder *moving* at the start of the takeaway, then he will get all the shoulder turn and hip turn necessary for a fine swing. If he leaves that left shoulder behind at the takeaway, then he will *only be making a hand-and-arm hit* and losing the advantage of his heavier, stronger physique.

Chunky players tend to pull themselves off balance by overuse of the hands and arms at the start of the backswing. Most often this results in infusing a "lunge" action instead of a swing when returning to the ball.

The basic problem lies in the fact that a heavy-set player naturally displaces much weight. Also, it's difficult for him to execute a proper midriff-turning action. This is what makes him inclined to sway off the ball to the right, and "lunge" forward on the downswing, causing topping, hitting behind the ball and loss of distance. For this reason, the chunky player should take a slightly wider stance than normal to brace himself against an overshifting of weight. Also, by proper use of the shoulders, he will find it easier to stay over the ball.

Sometimes the chunky player slides his weight to the right on the backswing and *fails to return it* to the address position at impact. This means his hands and arms will lead the body through the ball, closing the clubface and causing a pulled shot. Again, proper use of the shoulders and a wide stance should help prevent this fault.

Another factor the heavy-built player should be aware of is that his arc of swing is appreciably shorter than that of the slim, tall golfer. This puts him closer to the hitting area than the tall player and gives him less time to develop needed clubhead speed. The chunky player can overcome this problem by doing two things: adding right forearm punch as he comes into the hitting area (mentioned above) and swinging at a slightly faster tempo than the taller player.

The player of average height and build has none of the limitations of the chunky or the tall, slim golfer. He has adequate strength and is supple enough to make the necessary 90-degree turn with the shoulders on the backswing. He should use what is called the "classic" swing.

This classic swing is a perfect blending of two elements: the rotational or turning action of the body and the upward and downward hand and arm action.

7

The swing starts with a slight raising of the left heel, causing the left side of the body to take charge. The raising of the left heel and the bending of the left knee start the pivoting action, in which the right side of the body is forced around behind the player's head. The arms and hands meanwhile swing upward in front of the body to the top of the swing.

The downswing is started by returning the left heel firmly to the ground. The arms and hands strike downward and blend automatically to send the ball flying.

The player using the classic swing must guard against swinging too upright or too flat. If he goes too upright, he will be using a hands-and-arms swing without the height and reach that only a tall player possesses. If he goes too flat, he will be using a shoulder swing without the necessary bulk or muscle that only the heavy-set player has. As a rough guide, the player of average build should ensure that at the top of the swing his club shaft lies *midway between the point of the right shoulder and the base of the neck.* This position assures him the correct blend of rotational body action and hand-and-arm action.

A word on the proper equipment. If you are extremely tall, then clubs of average lie and length will not do. You should purchase clubs that are a little longer than normal—unless your arms are exceptionally long in relation to the rest of your body—and definitely those with an upright lie. (This means that when the club is soled flat on the ground the shaft will be more nearly vertical than the club of medium lie.)

If you're short and chunky, then you must use clubs that have a flat lie. You can often increase the width of your swing by using clubs as much as two inches longer than standard. However, guard against getting clubs much longer than that. The longer the length of shaft, the more difficult it becomes to control the club.

Whatever your height and build, remember that the lie of the club is just as important as the length, because it sets up the *correct swing plane* for the individual player. Your golf professional is the right man to advise the proper selection of length and lie for your particular physique.

Perhaps the most important point about this whole discussion of the different swings for the various physical types is that a player should not assume, once having learned the swing, *that this action will be the right one for him to use for the rest of his life.*

Walter Hagen started playing golf with the classic swing. Some years later, when he had put on weight, he would dominate the swing with shoulder action and punch the ball with the hands and arms. Take Lawson Little, too. He had a classic swing at the time he won the U.S. and the British Amateur championships in two successive years. Shortly thereafter, he gained weight and adopted the slugging techniques of the chunky players.

Golf teachers and parents should pay particular attention to the swings of youngsters as they grow up. Some will grow very tall and slender and should make adjustments to the upright method of swinging. Others will tend to become portly, or heavy and muscular, and should look to the shoulder method of swinging to get the best out of their build.

What swing are you built for?

Grip Left and Right

by Marty Cromb

Everyone agrees that the grip is the most fundamental and important part of golf, and yet so much unnecessary technical instruction is written that the average player winds up so confused he can't possibly hold the club properly. Actually, all you need do is position your thumbs correctly and you can't help but have a proper grip. Work from an imaginary center line that runs down the top center of the shaft. Position your left hand so that the left side of the left thumb is just to the right of that center line. Place your right hand snug on the left with the right thumb just to the left of the center line. That's all there is to it. I might also add that you hear a great deal about putting on the pressure with the last three fingers of the left hand and the thumb and forefinger of the right hand. Just remember this: None of your fingers should be idle passengers. So position your thumbs properly and the other fingers will fall in line naturally. Finally, be absolutely certain to check your grip *after* your swing to ascertain whether you have unconsciously changed your grip at some point during the address or swing as so many players do.

Line Up Left

by Bill De Angelis

A common fault of many golfers who find they are hitting the ball to the right of their target is poor alignment. The player having this difficulty usually positions himself at address so that his left shoulder is pointing at the pin. Actually, the line of flight runs from the ball to the pin, and when lining up the left shoulder at the pin, the golfer in reality is lining up his body to the right of his target. To position yourself properly, place your club behind the ball and *visualize with your eyes a line from the ball to the pin.* Your body should then be *parallel to this line and your left shoulder will point to the left of the target.* The correct inside-outside swing will then give you a straight hit, directly at the green. The secret of proper alignment is keeping the two imaginary lines parallel. So remember, have your left shoulder point to the left of the pin if you want to hit your ball straight at the pin.

LEFT SHOULDER

LINE OF FLIGHT

13

Split the Flag

by Brian Halpenny

Most golfers are too concerned with taking the club back, with the unfortunate result that they do not know what to do once they get it there. The point is, *what you do when and after you hit the ball is far more important than what you do on the takeaway.* By stressing the backswing, not enough attention is given to keeping the swing going forward. Here is where proper movement can provide great accuracy as well as consistency. And it is something that can be executed on the practice tee or the driving range. Initially, the downswing, much over-simplified, is a move to the left, with the shoulders and head held behind the shot. Once the ball is struck, your club shaft at the halfway position of the follow-through should *line up with the pin or the middle of the fairway.* In other words, by the time your hands reach shoulder height, the club should be vertically on line with the target, and ideally split the flag. If you can get your club to this position repeatedly, you're on your way to success.

14

Start with a Waggle

by Stuart Murray

To begin a swing, cultivate a waggle. Therein lies the start of your swing. You cannot adequately start a swing at the ball from a dead position, as it were. *A waggle should not be performed aimlessly, but by conscious control and application of power with the hands and fingers. Move the clubhead backward and, then, move it forward, thinking only of producing a swing. This gives the necessary feel with the hands of the clubhead and consciousness of an increasing control of its movements. As a player becomes more proficient, he will continue to waggle into a complete backward and forward swing.* Many great players in different sports have featured a fine waggle—Snead, Ruth, Williams, Spahn, etc. Sandy Herd, who was one of Scotland's great golfers, had over 21 waggles, and when at one time he was asked to reduce the number during a filming of his swing, hit the ball poorly. So they switched on the cameras at 17 waggles to get the picture, and Sandy was just fine.

Relax for the Big Hit

by Sam Sharrow

All those golfers who look to muscle tension for the "big hit," and still haven't found it, have been looking in the wrong place. If anything, muscle tension prevents a good strong hit and only multiplies errors. To begin with, a stiff left arm at address invariably means a rigid grip that, in turn, prevents cocking your wrists. Consequently, the club is lifted instead of swung on the takeaway, the body doesn't turn enough and the backswing is incomplete. From the top of the swing, those stiff arms and wrists can only throw the club, or "fly-cast," forcing you to cut across the ball. Since the wrists were never cocked to begin with, there's no possible way to release the club. Instead of tensing, keep the left arm extended— but relaxed! On the forward swing, as in baseball, turn the left side toward and away from the hole. Although the left side is firm, it must not be locked on target. The idea is to *turn!* Any attempt to hit with stiff arms freezes the left side, making correct weight shift and hand action impossible. So, for that "big hit," *relax*.

GOOD DOWNSWING BAD

GOOD   BACKSWING   BAD

19

Keep the Head Still

by Benito L. Lueras

Keeping the head still (not stiff) during the golf swing is one of the more challenging tasks for beginners to learn and for golfing addicts to remember. The following is advice that I have found most effective with my students. To be fair, head movement is definitely more difficult to detect than it is to correct. Usually, the golfer, involved as he is in his own swing, is quite unaware of such motion and, therefore, is justifiably unable to note it. To mark his movement the golfer needs a reference point. I suggest that you try this: Roll up a sheet of paper, place it in your mouth, point it at the ball and swing. If there is any head movement, the eye will catch it because the pointer will move, showing you just how much and where you moved your head. Practice swinging the club, keeping the pointer aimed directly at the ball or at a spot on the grass or rug. Once you have learned to detect the error you will be able to make the necessary adjustments to keep your head under control.

The Trunk Line to Control

by Rick Liljedahl

Most golfers are well aware of how important it is not to sway. Well, for the sake of control and consistency, it is just as important that the trunk of the body (from the hips to the head) remain at the same angle throughout the swing as it is at address. If the trunk is raised on the backswing, you top the ball; if it lowers on the way down, you hit behind the ball. Concentrate on keeping the trunk steady through the hitting zone. You can acquire this feeling by keeping your head as free of movement as you possibly can. Swing the club through the impact zone, riveting your head behind the spot where the ball was teed. As the club passes through this area, throw the clubhead out toward the target, allowing your hands to come to a high finish. This "hands high" action encourages an inside-out pattern in your swing. The steady trunk keeps the arc consistent, bringing the club along the same path on which it went back. Do this and you will observe both finer control and greater distance on all your wood shots.

TOPPED
(IF YOU RAISE UP)

DIG IN
(IF YOU DIP DOWN)

23

Don't Swing with a Sway

by John J. Gavins

Correct hand action is one of the most important elements in a sound golf swing. And hand action will be limited if a player allows his head to sway either on his backswing or follow-through. *The first place that sway occurs is in the backswing. The most common fault players have when they sway at this point in their swings is to allow the weight to roll on the outside edge of the right foot.* This allows the head to move laterally to the right, contributing to a sway. *To correct this, simply keep the weight on the inside edge of the right foot at address and make certain it remains there during the entire backswing.* This simple correction will eliminate sway in the backswing. When you sway on the follow-through, come to a complete halt at the finish of the swing and check your position. The golfer who sways will find his head forward of his stomach at the finish of his swing. *The correction is to finish your swing with your stomach ahead of your head.* This will allow the hands to work better throughout the swing.

25

Transfer Your Weight

by Frank Boynton

Teaching golfers not to leave their full weight on the left side during the backswing and on the right side on the downswing, instead of vice versa, which is the proper movement, has been my main concern on the practice tee lately. I think this fault is as common as moving too much to the right on the takeaway. Both, however, are body-sway mistakes. The proper weight transfer should never be confused with body sway. When you take the club back correctly, you should find, at the top of the backswing, that *your left knee is flexed and pointing behind the ball*. The weight should be on your right leg, inside the right foot, and *your head directly over the ball*. Most important, there will be no stiffness in your right knee and no overpowering exertion or strain in the upper body. Now you are ready to move your left hip laterally and hit into a firm left side, something that you would find impossible to do otherwise. All movements will be smoother, the results better and the game of golf a lot easier.

Lupo

WEIGHT

CORRECT

X

WEIGHT

INCORRECT

27

For a Good Grip—Start to Pray

by Nick Martino

Practically all of the beginning golfers I've taught came to me with great concern about the golf grip. They felt that properly placing the hands on the shaft had to be one of the most difficult, if not impossible, things in the game to learn.

The root of the problem had to do with their useless worry over the exact placement of each finger on the golf club. This preoccupation with individual parts of the grip prevented them from perceiving the true purpose of the grip. When you perform the most ordinary of tasks with the hands, you use them correctly—without thinking. For example, picking up a fork, or a pencil off the desk. *Control already exists!*

The most important single element to know about the golf grip is the *why* of it. The golfer first must have a good idea about what the relationship is between the grip and the swing itself. The golf grip's primary function is to hold the club and permit the clubhead to swing in a free-flowing motion without any interference from the grip-end of the golf club. For this reason, I would like to state here that I prefer to say "hold" the club rather than grip the club.

Experience has taught me that the word *grip* psychologically implies excessive pressure to the golfer. It is this pressure that destroys sensitivity in the fingers, without which it is impossible to swing the club properly. When the word grip is repeatedly mentioned, the student will unconsciously tighten his fingers on the shaft of the club. The golfer must first learn that you simply hold the club, nothing more, nothing less. Once the student latches on to this idea he is well on his way to a good golf game.

With the meaning of the grip firmly established in your mind, the way you form the grip is really the simplest of all things to learn in the game of golf. And remember, the grip with the most natural feeling is the best grip for you.

The only "must" I give my pupils is that the basic position of the hands be correct. I strongly feel that whether you overlap, interlock or use the 10-finger grip, the palms still should oppose each other. The reason is that the hands must be in perfect balance to allow the clubhead to swing freely.

I sometimes use the image of a person praying. The palms first oppose each other, then the only difference from the prayer position is that the right is placed below the left. To hit the ball far and straight, the palms must face each other because the golf club is swung backward and forward and not in any other direction.

If the basic position of the hands is other than the palms facing each other, then some compensatory movement must take place during the swing. What you have then is an error correcting an error. You might hit an occasional good shot, but never a series of consecutive perfect shots.

Grips can and do differ as much as personalities. No two persons' hands look exactly alike on the golf club, and you shouldn't try to force your grip to look like someone else's. If there were only one way to hold the golf club, you wouldn't have so many great golfers using different grips.

Let's take a look at some of the grips and why they are used. The most popular is the Vardon or overlapping grip. The palms still oppose each other, but in this case, the little finger of the right hand wraps around the knuckle of the index finger of the left hand. The reason is simple. You take one finger off the shaft because the right hand is usually stronger than the left. This prevents the right from overpowering the left.

With the interlocking grip, the principal or index finger of the left hand is taken off the shaft, making the weaker hand weaker. Therefore, in most instances it is unwise for a naturally right-handed person to further weaken the left. Now, if the golfer were left-handed and in fact had a very strong left, it would be advisable for this person to interlock, to equalize the strength in both hands.

It would also follow that if a person had equal strength and feel in both hands to start with, the golfer should try the 10-finger grip (all fingers on the shaft). Art Wall and Bob Rosburg, two of the tour's better players in past years, used this grip with great success. What I am saying is that the function of different kinds of grips is to make both hands work as one unit—not one hand against the other.

A question that is often posed by my students is, "What effect does tension of the hands have on the way a golf ball is hit?" My answer is that any interference by either the left or right hand will prevent the clubhead from doing its intended job. Too much pressure exerted by the fingers of the left hand will force the club outside its natural path—for example, an outside-in action which causes a shank, slice or fade, depending on the amount of added pressure applied.

Conversely, too much pressure by the fingers of the right hand will result in a snap-hook, pull or slight draw for the same reason stated above. Again, equal pressure of a controlled kind is what's needed for the clubhead to perform as it should.

Summing up, now, I would like the reader to take away with him this one thought about the golf grip: Don't violate the rule of naturalness, because the ultimate contribution of the grip, or as I like to put it, "holding the club," is to permit the clubhead to swing in the purest definition of the word *swing*.

II. THE SWING

Ernest Jones used to preach "swing the clubhead." Harry Obitz and Dick Farley use "the swing's the thing" as their teaching theme. And the chances are your local club pro tells his pupils to swing at the ball instead of lunging at it. All this emphasis on the word "swing" isn't accidental, because that's precisely what you must do in order to play this game competently. The backswing simply sets the tempo and gets you into position to hit the ball, but most players are so eager to lash the ball great distances that they jerk the club back so fast they have no chance to make a proper stroke. The following section not only will show you that you don't hit the ball with the backswing, but also it will show you how you *should* hit it— or should we say "swing" at it?

What Does a Good Swing "Feel" Like?

Literally hundreds of books and magazine articles have been written in the last 50 years or so about the mechanics of the golf swing, and more of the same continues to roll off the presses almost every day, which leads one to conclude that the only people who aren't proficient at the game are rank beginners or those who can't read.

If all these treatises were laid end to end they would stretch from Pine Valley to Prestwick, and yet, incredibly, the vast majority of golfers still can't break a hundred.

Admittedly, no two people do things the same way, and every golfer has to adjust his game to suit age, physical limitations, size, etc. But these modifications are relatively minor, and it can be said that, basically, there is only one correct way to swing a club. Assuming, then, that every golfer who has made any effort at all knows the fundamentals of the swing, it must be concluded that the cause of all those double and triple bogeys lies elsewhere.

Faced with a pupil who knows how to swing but can't do so properly, most teachers diagnose the problem as mental. This is getting closer to the source, but even here the ground is treacherous. Obviously, the mental side of golf is as important as the physical, but the golfer is prone to approach the subject from the wrong angle.

Many golfers blame their troubles on lack of concentration, but in an effort to do something about it they concentrate so hard that they become tense and have no chance of executing a correct swing. Apparently, then, the cure isn't to think about the shot, it is *not* to think about it. In other words, they should "feel" the shot.

To develop feel, the golfer must build a muscular memory through constant repetition of the correct movements. Now, there is nothing new in this theory and, in fact, there probably isn't a golfer alive who doesn't know that he must practice the right moves over and over in order to develop what has come to be called a repeating swing. However, knowing he must do it and knowing how to do it are two different things.

The object is to get some kind of mental image of what must be done, an image that can be called to mind time after time until the correct movement is automatic. This device must not be confused with consciously thinking about the shot, because if the golfer tries to think about how he is going to hit the ball he becomes tense, steers the ball or commits any one of a dozen other unpardonable sins.

The first place to start learning about feel is, obviously, with the grip, because if the golfer doesn't have the right idea at the beginning, he is irrevocably lost. Bob Toski likes to remind the pupil to grip the club as if he were a doctor holding a surgical instrument. He has always stressed a light grip, but this specific image was developed the day he actually gave a lesson to a surgeon. The doctor stepped up to the ball and took a stranglehold on the club, and Toski quickly called a halt. "You have to remember," he said, "that you are a 180-pound man swinging a 14-ounce club. The club isn't going to swing you. What would happen if you gripped a surgical instrument that way during an operation?"

The doctor immediately got the image, and so should you. The next time you take a death grip on the club, stop a moment and imagine how you would feel if a surgeon approached your appendix in such a fashion. Pretty frightening, isn't it?

Obviously, you can't stand up to the ball as loose as a dish rag—a certain firmness is essential—but the light grip will keep tension out of the hands and arms. Without this relaxed feeling in the upper body, you can't take the club back slow and easy. On the other hand, there should be a feeling of tension in the legs. It is the theory of John Jacobs, a well-known Briton, that there should be tension from the hips down to the feet. "Indeed," he has written, "I feel as though the top half of my body, which is at rest, is secured to a bottom half prepared for violent action. I feel as though I am sitting on top of a spring-system."

The next step is the pivot, and for this the best device is one used with great success by the late Percy Boomer, a famed British teacher whose book *On Learning Golf* is a must for anyone desiring to acquire feel. Boomer told the pupil to imagine he was standing in a barrel, hip high and wide enough to be just free of each hip, but a close enough fit to allow no movement except the pivot. This is perhaps the easiest image of all to conjure, and if you try it the next time you start your swing, you should quickly eliminate sway as well as any squatting or dipping motion.

The area between the takeaway and the top of the backswing doesn't readily lend itself to imagery, but it is important that you have some

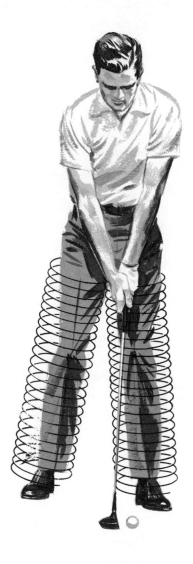

At address, you should feel as if the upper half of your body were poised on the top of a spring system. Any useful tension is felt not in the hands or arms, but in the coiled readiness for violent action that extends from the feet into the hips.

The barrel image, taught by Percy Boomer, is a mental device for obtaining the proper pivot and preventing sway.

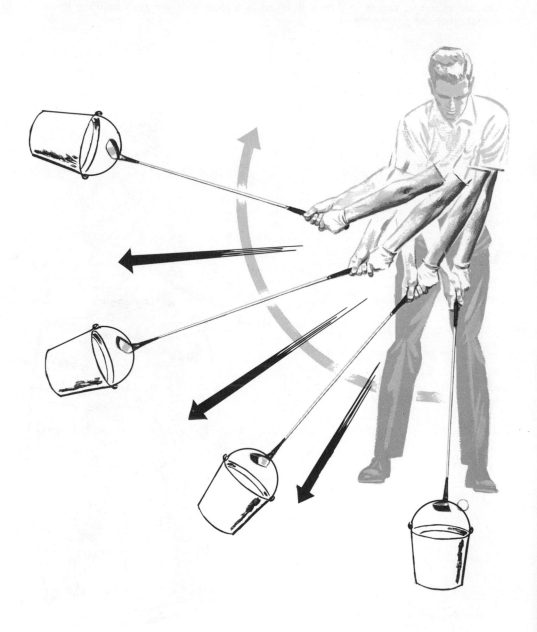

To keep the left arm fully extended for maximum arc and maximum clubhead
speed at impact, try to imagine that a weighted object, such as a pail of water,
is hanging from the hosel. The imagined pull should be enough to keep the left
arm straight.

sense of what must be done. The object, of course, is to keep the arms fully extended. Only in this way will the clubhead describe the maximum arc and thus attain maximum speed at impact. So, in order to keep the arms extended, try to imagine that the clubhead is a fairly heavy object that is exerting enough pull to keep the left elbow from bending. Don't worry about cocking your wrists; that will take care of itself as you near the top of the backswing. If, as a youngster, you ever spun around holding a pail of water straight out from your waist, you will recall that centrifugal force kept the water from spilling and also exerted enough pull to keep your arms extended. That is essentially the feeling you should have during the backswing until the hands are at least waist level.

Now we reach the most critical area: the end of the upward motion and the beginning of the downward motion, the part of the swing that separates the pro from the weekender. It is a popular notion that there is a pause at the top of the backswing, but that just isn't so. There is an instant, of course, between the time the clubhead stops going one way and starts going another, but during that brief time the weight has already begun to shift to the left side. If the golfer were to come to a complete stop at the top, the rhythm of the swing would be broken. He would probably wind up hitting from the top (starting the downswing with the hands and arms), and all would be lost.

The best way to get through this delicate phase is to employ a favorite theory of Joe Novak in which he compares the golf swing to the baseball swing. If you have played much baseball or have studied batting styles closely, you will recall that just as the hitter starts to stride into the pitch he pulls the bat back a little farther. Thus, while the body is moving in one direction, the bat is moving in the other, creating a stretching effect that allows him to lash at the ball with maximum power. The movements in the golf swing are no different; just before the clubhead reaches the end of the line on the backswing, the left heel goes down and the weight starts over to the left. This creates the springlike action that enables Mickey Mantle to hit 450-foot home runs and Jack Nicklaus to hit 300-yard drives.

The next time you're on the practice tee, give the baseball theory a try. Take a reasonably slow backswing to give yourself a chance to get into the proper position. Then, an instant before the backswing is completed, imagine you are a batter stepping into a pitch—start the weight shifting to the left side and feel that left arm stretch out. Don't worry about getting your body too far out in front. The clubhead will catch up at impact, and when it does it will be moving at a speed that should result in considerably longer drives.

There is still one more image that should be a part of your mental arsenal, and that is the feeling that you are hitting from inside out. Everyone with a knowledge of the fundamentals knows that the club must be taken back inside the intended line of flight. However, on the downswing, many golfers think they must consciously try to swing the club right down that line. Unless you are one of those rare golfers who can get away with swinging the club straight back and straight down, this "steering" of the shot will produce dreadful consequences. In order to get the desired result, you must (as the accompanying illustration shows) get the feeling that you are trying to hit the ball out to the right. The ball won't go that way, of course, but you must imagine that it will.

Driving square through the ball is more easily accomplished by following the stronger image of hitting the ball out to the right.

Obviously, you can't start out calling up all these images at once, but working on them one at a time—or stressing the ones that apply to particularly vexing parts of your swing—should produce gratifying results in short order.

This type of mental exercise is designed to remove the golfer's fear of the ball. Everybody's practice swing looks like Sam Snead's, but when the golfer steps up to the ball he comes unglued. However, by getting an image of how the swing should be executed and calling it to mind repeatedly until the movement is automatic, you can forget about hitting the ball and devote your attention to the matter of making a correct swing.

As Percy Boomer said, "You must learn to feel the sensations through your intellect and then forget them intellectually and leave them to your muscular memory."

Don't think about hitting the shot, just feel it.

Right Angle for Full Turn

by Don Clarkson

There was a time in my golf career when I couldn't make a full hip turn on the backswing, which, in effect, reduced both my shoulder turn and distance. I mentioned this to Bob Goalby one day and, after watching my swing, Bob noticed my left knee kicking almost straight ahead on the backswing. It was all caused by the angle of my left foot to the line of flight; and a contributing factor was my right foot, which was held square to the line. A simple move in my stance made all the difference. *I turned my left foot inward to the right and turned my right foot out a little so that both feet were at the same approximate angle* (see illustration). This new stance gave me more freedom to turn, and on the way back my left knee now flexed behind the ball instead of shooting straight out as before. As a result, with maximum shoulder turn, I was swinging easier and actually hitting the ball farther. So, if you feel you are having difficulty turning, my advice to you is to check your stance for correct foot angles. Pattern your stance after the "after" position in the illustration and you'll surely harness that full turn for maximum effort.

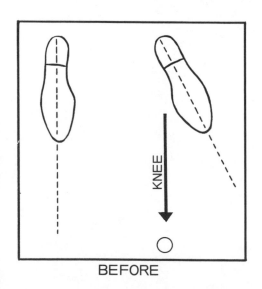

BEFORE

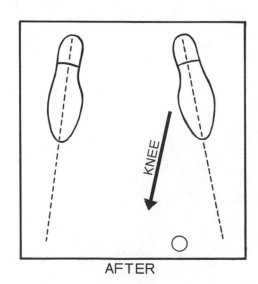

AFTER

Sweep It Back Low

by Tom Shaw

The golfer who picks up his driver on the takeaway rather than sweeping the club back low to the ground weakens his chances of hitting the ball long and straight. This is not always a fault of the average golfer. It happens to professionals, too. Joe Carr and I travel a lot together on the tour, and a while back Joe was having a tough time with his tee shots. Like a lot of weekenders, he was picking the club up. In trying to give him a reference checkpoint, I came up with what we called the "freckle" theory. Noticing that Joe had a freckle on the upper part of his left arm, I simply told him that he would be able to get started correctly if he were to take the club back "with your freckle." By concentrating on the freckle, Joe learned, or relearned, to sweep the club back, allowing his left shoulder to come under his chin on the backswing, from which point his upper body was coiled for the big hit. Now I realize that all golfers do not have a freckle to refer to, but the same sweep-back theory can work as nicely for you. This low move gets your left shoulder under your chin at the top of the backswing as shown in the illustration.

Shift, Overshift, Sway

by Jim Fogertey

One of golf's many problems arises from the too-conscious effort at shifting the weight on the backswing. More often than not, the shift is exaggerated. To make sure that he turns, the golfer tends to lift the left heel much too high, which throws the weight to the outside of the right foot and forces both body and head to move off the ball. The combination of these errors produces that *sway* from which it is almost impossible to recover. Thus, he is out of position when he reaches the ball on the downswing. To cure the overshift, first keep the weight in the middle of your stance at address. Then the proper shoulder turn on the backswing can easily be accomplished by holding the weight on the inside of your right foot on the backswing. As a result, it becomes virtually impossible to sway, and since the sway is nothing more than *a lateral movement to the right,* what you do is turn—*not with your whole body but with your shoulders*. In addition, you'll make a pleasant discovery: You needn't worry about shifting back when you start the downswing. That will take care of itself.

INCORRECT
WEIGHT
OUTSIDE

CORRECT
WEIGHT
INSIDE

Keep It All Together

by Art Decko

The goal of most golfers is a fluid, one-piece swing—one that is a repeating mechanism and functions the same way every time. A gimmick or mental thought that I use to help my students put all the elements of a golf swing together is the hands–left knee theory. *From the top, I try to get the player to think of coordinating the movement of the hands with the left knee.* If the hands start to move before the left knee, I find the player will be too early with the clubhead and will pull or snap-hook the ball. If the action of the left knee starts too soon, the hands will be late, knocking the ball to the right of the line, or worse, a slice. *As you begin the downswing, work on starting the left knee and the hands simultaneously so that hands and clubhead will arrive at impact together. By* keeping this image in your mind, you should be getting it all together in very short order.

Get Off on the Right Foot

by Jim Foulis

Most golfers quit on a shot because of poor footwork. That is, they don't get the right side around fast enough because they stay on the right heel too long in the downswing. I teach the execution of the downswing by emphasizing the right-foot action rather than turning the left hip. I don't mean to imply that one is more important than the other, because the well-coordinated golfer turns his left hip into the swing at precisely the same instant he lifts his right heel. However, most golfers more quickly grasp the idea of initiating the downswing by pushing off with the right heel and forgetting about the left side. When a golfer is slow getting his right heel off the ground it usually proves he is exaggerating the action of the left heel in the backswing. That is, he lifts the left heel too high, throws himself off balance going back and isn't in a position to redeem himself by pushing off properly with the right heel on the downswing.

Delay the Climb-over

by Mike Krak

Everybody wants to hit the wood shots—whether from tee or fairway—with solid power. The general teaching theory is that you should hit the ball with the back of your left hand as the wrists snap through and then break. *I hold that there should be no wrist break until after the hands have reached eye level. The hands and arms should continue on through the hitting area in one straight piece.* A parallel is the manner in which a good tennis player keeps the wrist and arm firm in hitting a driving backhand. There is no wrist break. Look at the picture of almost any top professional—Jack Nicklaus and Arnold Palmer are top examples—and you will see that at eye level on the follow-through the wrist still is in a straight line with the arm, and the last three knuckles of the left hand are pointed back along the line of flight. (Palmer does it so much that the back of his left hand is toward the hole in his backswing.) *So for that extra distance, keep the back of the left hand going right out toward the hole until it is at eye level, and keep the hands and arms in one straight piece all the way through the hitting area.* Keep the left hand driving toward the hole. *Don't break wrists until eye level on your follow-through.*

The Myth of the Baseball Swing

by Joe Novak

Foremost among the many fallacies that have made golf confusing and unnecessarily difficult for too many people is the contention that golf is unlike any other sport. This attitude is expressed most clearly in a commonly used remark when criticism is directed at a struggling golfer's shots. The crack that is always made is, "You have too much of a baseball swing." Actually, nothing could be farther from the truth, because a baseball swing and a golf stroke are absolutely alike—alike in purpose and alike in execution. Both endeavors are doublehanded maneuvers wherein the player is developing an energy in or on a bat or a club, and is applying that bat or club to a ball.

The golfer has a much easier task, however, because he is attacking a quiet, sitting ball, while the ballplayer is being confronted with a whistling curve, an offspeed pitch, or one of several other devilish, deceitful deliveries.

Recently, Willie Mays was congratulated on how far he could drive a golf ball and, at the same time, was asked if he had found any difficulty hitting a golf ball. "Why, no," Mays answered, "there is no difficulty hitting a golf ball. Why should there be? The ball is just sitting there waiting for you to smack it." Outside of the fact that the golf stroke is applied to a still ball while the baseball swing must meet a moving, twisting ball, the operation is exactly alike.

The one thing that must be understood in this discussion is that the basis of control is entirely in the body. There is nothing new or different in this contention, because the "trick" of athletics is body control. There is really no power per se in an arm or a leg. True, one can toss a ball by using only the arm, but to really throw, one must use the body and get behind the throw.

The most striking example of the need for body control was demonstrated by the Southern California football team of 1940. This was a fine, powerful team, but they just could not kick goal after touchdown, so they decided "to beat the gun" by developing a kicker who could boot the ball from a standing position. Undoubtedly this worked nicely in practice, but under the pressure of the game the kicker seemed to freeze and was unable to perform. In short order U.S.C. was back to the conventional step and walk into the kick, which enabled the kicker to get his body into and behind the movement—all of which produced a consistent and powerful performance and once again there was calm and serenity on Bovard Field.

In the golf stroke as well as the baseball swing there are two movements. There is an upswing or a windup, and there is the downswing or delivery.

The upswing is definitely a right-handed, right-sided movement that requires a balance on the right foot, and the downswing is an equally definite left-handed, left-sided movement that requires a balance on the left foot. In short, footwork is the key to good golf and footwork is the key to consistent hits and home runs.

Let me digress for a moment to the other end of the action, the hands. As the golfer or the ballplayer is using the right arm and the right side to wind up, the left hand and left arm are providing valuable aid and assistance, not only in determining just how the club or the bat is being cocked or set in position. On the downswing, or delivery, things change completely, and here, as the left arm and left side take over and pull the club or the bat into the ball, the right arm and right hand are right there, not only to keep the club or bat in steady position but to provide that terrific punch or thrust of power at the moment of impact.

This double-barreled action of the hands will occur naturally and easily, but only if the body, the base of the action, is functioning properly—and the body will not function properly or effectively unless properly balanced.

Balance is arrived at through the simple process of using one's legs properly. For example, right-handed people always stand on their right foot and left-handed people always on their left foot. It is just a case of shifting one's weight to one leg or the other, depending simply on what action is being attempted.

Boxers are said to be through when their legs are gone, which means they cannot hit because they no longer have the strong legs upon which to balance themselves in order to deliver a blow.

No offense to Zsa Zsa Gabor is meant by relating this incident, but she once was asked to throw out the baseball at the opening game of the

Here is Mickey Mantle at the optimum point in the windup.

In the delivery the left hand and side take over. Mickey pulls the bat into the ball.

Mantle takes the bat back with the right side similar to the way Tom Weiskopf reaches the top of the backswing. In both cases the left hand and arm keep the bat and club in the proper position.

The first move in the downswing is the same as Mantle's. Along with a slight lateral movement of the left hip there is a definite feeling of pulling the left hand into the shot.

Mickey here has stepped into the ball and yet his wrists are still cocked.

The truth of a fine swing is apparent here when the bat is released.

Tom also has moved into the hitting area with the wrists cocked and the clubhead delayed to its fullest. In both instances the moving into the ball with hands in a cocked position provides the great power both men create at impact.

No different than the swinging of a bat, the release of the clubhead at precisely the right moment with the greatest amount of power possible is the result of coordinating fine hand action with body movement.

55

season. Zsa Zsa grasped the ball and actually threw it behind her into the crowd instead of forward onto the playing field. Zsa Zsa just was not prepared, she just was not properly balanced to make the throw. And so it is with all people who are untrained athletically—they are just not balanced for the task at hand.

The batter, in most cases, assumes a wound-up position at the plate. He balances himself on his right foot, cocks or contracts his right arm and draws his right foot back and away from the plate, which gives him a sort of windup of his right side. Then, from this dead-still, wound-up position, he strides forward onto his left foot and into the ball with the correct and proper action of a backhand stroke, wherein the left side and the left arm take the lead.

There are many golfers who address the golf ball in the same way. They balance themselves on their right foot and raise the club to the top of the swing, and even as this windup is being completed they begin to go into a stride onto the left foot, where they must be in order to make the natural, powerful stroke onto the ball. The outstanding example of taking this style of starting position in golf was Gene Littler. And this style is quite common with today's golfers, particularly those who practice the one-piece golf-swing theory.

The classical golf swing is one wherein the player addresses the ball with his weight on his left foot—his starting position is exactly the same as the position he will be in at impact, that is, balanced on the left foot. This is a perfectly natural position to assume and it is helpful because it gives the player a sense and feeling of just where he should be at impact.

This is a natural position. The logical place to play the golf ball in all shots is opposite the left foot because that is where the player will be at impact, balanced on the left foot, and that is where the swing will automatically center. This placement of the ball and club opposite the left foot at address, and the fact that the right hand is always placed at a lower position than the left on the club shaft, causes the player to relax the right knee slightly, and this causes the balance or weight shift over to the left foot.

However, as long as the weight is kept on the left foot, it becomes most difficult, in fact, very unnatural to raise the club to the top of the swing (and I state this emphatically in spite of those who insist the left heel should be glued to the ground at all times during a golf swing). But with a perfectly natural forward press action—a distinctive one-two,

56

zigzag motion that is common practice with all top-notch performers—the player reverses his knee positions at the start of the downswing and thus rebalances himself on his left foot so that he can come onto and through the ball with full force.

The above is the classical procedure in golf and it is the only way to have a full, free motion on both upswing and downswing. This is the style and procedure that made Bobby Jones invincible. It is the style that made Jimmy Thomson the most consistent long hitter in golf and it is the style that has kept the Samuel Jackson Snead golf machine running so smoothly for these many years.

The ballplayer does not have time to go into any one-two forward press action, but despite this, the left-handed Babe Ruth and Ted Williams possessed classic swings that enabled them to get onto their right foot for the windup and still get niccly back on their left foot in time to sink the bat into and through the ball. A study of the batting form of Hank Aaron and Willie Mays reveals a similar procedure. At the exact time that the pitcher cocks his arm, both Aaron and Mays actually pick or lift their left foot off the ground (about an inch or so). This balances them on their right feet for the windup and they are all set to step right into the ball.

Ron Fairly has a similar mannerism and he was a red-hot performer at the start of one season. An injury kept Fairly side-lined, and when he returned to the line-up, his rhythm was gone. Careful observation by Walt Alston revealed that Fairly had assumed a very wide stance at the plate, and this had locked or tightened his legs to the extent that his batting swing was ineffective. Alston suggested a narrower stance, and in short order, Fairly was able to work his legs naturally and was soon back into another hot batting streak.

Golfers would do well to check their own stance, and despite Doug Sanders' remarkable success with his Colossus of Rhodes stance, it would be helpful to all golfers if they used a narrow one.

This chapter, it is hoped, should have led the reader to these conclusions:

There are two swings to every golf stroke, just as there are two to every baseball swing.

The upswing, or windup, in both cases is made with the right side of the body and the right arm, which requires a balance on the right foot, and the downswing and hit are done with the left side of the body, which calls for a balance on the left foot.

The golfer can actually take aim by striking from a position on his left foot and then, through the medium of the forward-press action, shift his balance to his right foot, from which point he can make a measured hit.

Or the golfer can use the modified form of balancing himself on his right foot, a form which has certain drawbacks in regard to club control.

The baseball player, although attacking a moving ball, swings from a similarly wound-up position, in which he times his action so that it coincides with the windup and delivery action of the pitcher.

Batter up!

III. THE LONG GAME

When the average golfer thinks of his long game, he thinks of his driver, because he has been conditioned to think in terms of distance. However, the long game also includes the fairway woods and long irons, and the duffer would do well to consider all these clubs. After all, none of us is a Jack Nicklaus or a Tom Weiskopf, who play most par-four holes with a drive and a wedge. Mr. Average, if he is lucky enough to hit one 200 yards down the middle, still has a wood or long iron to reach the green, and no amount of wishful thinking is going to change the situation. The first thing to do is to get rid of that pesky slice—or hook—and by the time you are hitting everything straight, chances are you'll be hitting the ball farther, too. The following sound advice, if heeded, will soon have you hitting your second shot with a four-iron from the fairway instead of a three-wood from the rough, and you'll be getting to the green in time to putt for birdies instead of bogeys.

A Cure for Golf's Common Cold

by Tom Nieporte

One of the major, constant and chronic ailments of golfers everywhere is the slice—that deceptive drive or iron shot that sounds well hit, jumps smartly off the face of the club, rises straight out for 100 yards or so, and then strangely, pathetically and fatally slides to the right and into trouble. Bananas are fine for simians and non-weight-watchers, but hardly the course diet for golfers. Therefore, the majority of my lessons during the year deal in varying ways with curing this all too common fault; and the following advice, based on this experience, should prove a successful means of correcting the slice.

First, since you don't hit the ball with your backswing, the club should be taken back slowly, with the hands and arms in coordination with the turning shoulders and hips. Once you reach the top of the backswing, a pertinent question to ask yourself is "What are the angles of my shoulders and of my hips?" Since this is the point at which a good or bad swing begins, the position at the top is of utmost concern.

On the full turn, *the tip of the left shoulder must be pointing at the ball, with the right shoulder higher than the left.* In other words, the line from left to right shoulder goes uphill. Obviously, the hips, too, are tilted or slanted on a similar but less severe angle, and the turn is about half that of the shoulders. That, in itself, is simple enough and most golfers to some extent do attain this position—this shoulder and hip relationship.

The biggest problem, however, arises as the golfer begins his downswing and comes into the proper hitting position behind the ball. Here is where many strange and unorthodox moves suddenly creep in, upstage the controlled takeaway and destroy what otherwise is a good backswing. But, barring the wrong moves, in classical terminology, what happens—or should happen—in the downswing is the following.

The first movement on the return is made by the hips. As the weight shifts to the left side, *the left hip moves out diagonally across the line of flight* (or at least you should have the feeling that it is happening this

At the top of the backswing, think about the angles of your shoulders and hips. The top of the left shoulder must be pointing at the ball, *left,* with the right shoulder higher than the left. The line from shoulder to shoulder, *right,* slants uphill, with the hip plane on a similar slant, only somewhat less severe.

way). *The hip then moves directly at the target and finally turns.* This sequence of movements occurs not as I have described it—in bits and pieces—but as one smooth, rhythmic motion. Merely turning the left hip out of the way (as most golfers phrase it) causes the average golfer or high-handicapper additional problems with his right shoulder motion on the downswing.

Following hard upon the weight shift is the action of the shoulders. They will move unconsciously and correctly—being pulled down and toward the ball—if no artificial or steering motion is attempted. In general, all during the downswing, the left shoulder is behind the left

61

In a smooth motion, the hips move to the left as the weight shifts (lower arrow), then roll diagonally across the line of flight (middle arrow), and then, finally, directly through at the target before turning.

The right shoulder doesn't come out and over the ball, but down and inside and out to the right of the line to the target. Visually, you should think of the right shoulder dropping down into your right pocket.

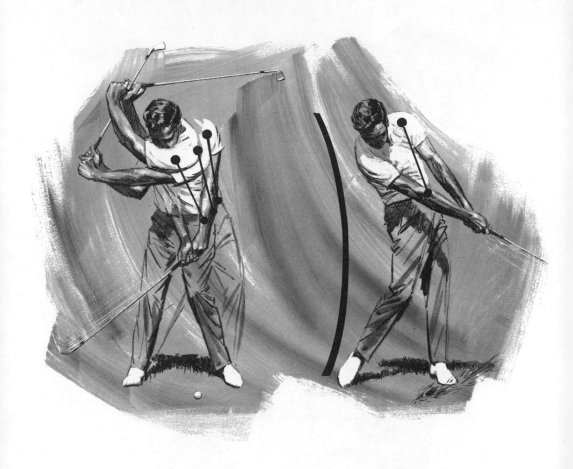

Make sure the left hip leads the downswing. At all times the left shoulder should be behind the left hip, *left,* so that a line drawn from shoulder to hip would slant slightly. To check on this initial shift of weight, your body should have a distinct bow to it, *right.*

hip—or, in other words, at all times during the downswing, the left hip is out in front of the left shoulder. As a sometime check on this initial shift of weight and hips, and the motion of the shoulders, you should find the body with a distinct bow to it.

From another point of view, the imagination, I have found the following pictorial advice to be quite helpful in overcoming the slice. Imagine, if you will, that your left arm is the hand of a clock (running backward) and is attached, as it were, by a cotter pin. What would happen if your left arm were suddenly to drop from twelve o'clock to six o'clock? That movement, although an exaggeration of the proper golf move, is approximate enough to give any golfer a vivid picture of what the arms, especially the leading left arm, should be doing on the downswing. Now try that "drop" motion with the club held only in the left hand with the shoulder point acting as the center of the clock and the fulcrum of this "drop." Observe that motion carefully. Beyond any doubt, the action is inside-out. It cannot be anything else. In addition, the idea of a clock is a good method of encouraging the head to remain behind the ball during the swing and to prevent it from bobbing up and down or swaying back and forth.

Remember, this picture is only a means to an end. The shoulder point does not really remain immovable or rigid. During the swing it does move, but only naturally, *not* with any attempt at steering the ball, and in direct response to the hip shift and the action of the right shoulder.

As for this action of the right shoulder, it is far from being an orphan during the downswing. It does not come out and over the ball, nor does it swing around. *It moves down and inside and out to the right of the line to the target.* Better yet, you should think of the right shoulder dropping into the right pocket. That is really the kind of motion you should be making.

Since the idea of all this is to teach the amateur to swing inside-out, here are two additional practice aids that ensure grooving an inside-out swing.

As a practice guide, prop up a handy object like a bench or a chair, with the ball placed beneath the forward end. Obviously, if you swing across the ball you must strike the bench or chair first with the club shaft. But, under the compulsion or need to avoid hitting the bench, you will be forced to swing inside-out and, surprisingly enough, the ball will probably be drawn from right to left.

A second practice guide is to take two golf balls, placing the first one in hitting position and the second about six to eight inches behind it but just to the outside of the intended line of flight. (In place of the second ball, you might put a pack of cigarettes or a head cover.) Address the forward ball and then take your normal swing. If you disturb the second ball on your return (and you will if you're a slicer), you will have proved your arc is outside-in or slice-prone. Although most golfers hit both balls at first, with enough practice, swinging as described before, you will have honed a fine inside-out swing that strikes only the forward ball and produces shots that go straight or draw slightly.

INSIDE OUT

INCORRECT

To practice the inside-out swing, take two golf balls, placing the first in hitting position and the second a few inches behind, just outside the line of flight. If you hit the second ball, you've swung outside-in, or slice-prone. Or put a ball under a bench and try to hit it without striking the bench first.

But, like anything else worth cultivating, merely reading about a slice cure will not turn the trick. You must get out on the practice tee and give what you have just read a real workout.

That's where all good repeating swings are made.

Two Inches for 20 More Yards

by Clarence Doser

A good tip for a golfer who wants to add distance to his tee shots without swinging harder is *to use clubs with extra long shafts. Longer shafts will give you a larger arc and add clubhead speed.* One inch added to the shaft is the equivalent of adding two inches to your height and four points to the club's swing weight. I suggest a driver with a 45-inch shaft instead of the normal 43-inch shaft. *A longer shaft will necessitate some changes in the swing. The swing will be flatter because you'll be standing farther from the ball and the angle of the shaft to the ground will be smaller. Don't overpower the ball, try "sweet-swinging" the club, relying more on rhythm and timing and less on punch. Also, wait for the clubhead at the top of the backswing before starting the downswing.* Once you've mastered the technique of swinging the longer club, you'll find that you can control the flight of the ball better, as well as add 20 yards or more to your drive.

Lead with the Hip

by Ralph Hutchison

This is an era in which everyone wants to be a power hitter. There is a "secret" to it. If you want to be a longer hitter the answer lies in *starting the backswing with the right hip and commencing the downswing with practically simultaneous power action in both feet.* It really isn't terribly complicated. The sequence is simplicity itself. If you will turn the right hip to begin the backswing and make the hands and arms follow it all the way to the top of the backswing, you will find that it keeps your right elbow tucked in against the side, where it belongs, and that also it has prevented you from picking up the club. Now you are in perfect position to deliver your power. How do you do this? *The left heel leads the action by planting itself firmly on the ground—while in the same motion the right heel comes up off the ground. Your left hand works with your left heel and as your right heel comes up the right leg straightens, putting the brake on the right side to keep it from overpowering the left side.* At this point you will discover that your hands and arms have been forced into the downswing in the perfect arc, with the right elbow tucked in where it should be, and you are ready to unleash your full power.

71

Splitting the Fairway

by Guy Wimberly

Nothing in golf rivals stepping to the tee and rifling the ball down the middle of the fairway. However, empirical evidence confirms that the average golfer all too often drives himself into trouble and, hence, unnecessary strokes. But with consistent, repetitive moves, any golfer should be able to split the fairways with regularity. To return the club as square at impact as it was at address, the position of the hands shortly after the takeaway should be a mirror image of the follow-through shortly after impact. This idea is best illustrated in terms of three handshaking positions: at address, takeaway and follow-through. If the right hand is moved into a handshaking position waist high in the backswing, starting from address, and similarly, if the handshaking position is achieved waist high in the follow-through, the clubhead should be square through impact. These three hand positions during the swing will assure you the correct square action through the hitting zone. And you never lose strokes down the middle.

Fairway Woods in the Wind

by Herman Barron

One of the more discouraging shots in golf is the fairway wood that lofts the ball swiftly into the air only to have the head wind blunt its thrust, leaving you well short of your intended position. Here is an occasion for that low stiletto shot, the kind of shot that will not leave the ball impaled helplessly on the wind. Instead, since the object is to keep the ball low, avoiding the high trajectory, *do not play the ball in its usual position—* off the left heel. I advise *moving the ball back more than you normally do toward the right foot.* This *does not mean* you should play the ball *off the right foot.* It is simply an adjustment that should be made in terms of an inch or three, but *never* back past the middle of the stance. There is no alteration in the swing aside from keeping the club low to the ground on the takeaway and returning in the same low arc. Grip the club slightly lower down the shaft in order to shorten your swing and increase your accuracy. On all such fairway shots, I would suggest that you take one club longer, further reducing the loft of the shot and redeeming the distance lost to the head wind. This will help you assert much more control without the feeling of hitting so hard.

No.3 WOOD

NORMAL

NORMAL

LOW

Use the Five-Wood

by Joe Capello

Before you decide that a five-wood is for ladies, keep in mind that many professionals carry this club in their bags. A five-wood is an extraordinarily valuable club for golfers, especially those of medium build and with a medium game in the high 80's or into the 90's. It can be used at different speeds, for full shots or punch shots, and it is much safer than the comparable iron, the three-iron. It has a great margin of error. For example, with other clubs, if you were to hit behind the ball, catching the turf first, you would have a badly missed shot. But if you were to do the same with a five-wood, you can still get results. It is also good in the rough. You can get to the ball with this club even where otherwise a five-iron might be the selection, because it has the length and the loft to cut a swath through the high grass. When using a five-wood, swing as you do with other woods. Play the ball off the left heel, take the club back slowly, and on the return to the ball, keep the club moving and let the weighted head carry you into a good follow-through. The beauty of this club is that you can even use it incorrectly and get results. That is, should you accidentally shut the face, you still will get at the ball. A long iron won't give this advantage.

Use Enough Stick

by Gus Norwich

Sit on the tee of any short or medium par-three hole and watch the next forty golfers hit their tee shots. Chances are that for every one whose ball stops past the cup, there'll be nineteen who are short—and many of them by as much as 20 or 30 yards. A high percentage of golfers with tolerably good swings seem to make it a habit to underclub themselves. Don't be ashamed to use more club than the long hitters if you need more. Observe, also, the vital fact that most tees and most greens are about 30 yards long. If you can carry the front of a green with a seven-iron from the front of the tee, you need a one-iron or a four-wood from the *back of the tee to the back of the green,* because the hole will play 60 yards longer, and irons are progressively 10 yards longer in normal carry from nine-iron to one-iron. Keeping this in mind, an 88-average shooter can lower his average to 82. Too many players use the same club for each round, regardless of location of tee markers or cup on any given par-three hole.

4 WOOD

4
IRON

Lupo

Leave the Driving to Your Subconscious

by Len Nobleman

One of my favorite playing companions at the Kleinburg Golf Club, located near Toronto, Canada, is Charlie Drouin. At present Charlie shoots in the 90's, but he carries with him the major ingredient for success at golf. I passed it on to him one Saturday afternoon when he came up to me and said, "Tell me, Len, what is the secret of your success?" I had just finished the front nine in 34, 2 under par, the last two holes played in almost total darkness, and I 3-putted that last hole. All right, you say, so what? The "what" is that four months earlier I couldn't break 50 on the same nine.

Sounds incredible, doesn't it? You know, I still can't believe it myself. Here I sit wondering where I am going to finish in golf. My handicap has dropped in just four months from 18 to 7 and it's still going down. What is the secret of my improvement? If I were to put it into a few words I would say this: "I have acquired a positive mental attitude in golf, which continues to develop at a fantastic rate. This mental attitude is not words, nor wishful thinking, it is a genuine part of me; it has been made so because of my excellent training in self-hypnosis."

Let's go back to the spring of 1966. At that time I was working in Detroit and was invited to participate in the industrial golf league. "Boy," I thought to myself, "am I going to show these guys!" After all, I had spent the entire winter pounding balls at the indoor driving range and my outdoor practice in the spring had shown my improvement. True, I still wondered if it was a permanent improvement, but I felt confident that I was on my way. But after chopping my way around a nine-hole course on which Mickey Mouse could break par, my score was 54 and my confidence was gone.

It was at this point that I made up my mind to sell my clubs and take up knitting. I don't know what it is about golf that intrigues one, but before I could throw the clubs away I just had to try something I had been thinking about for some time. I looked in the Detroit telephone directory and called Hyman Lewis, director of the Lewis Hypnosis Center in Oak Park, Michigan, a certified hypno-technician. "Can hypnosis improve my golf game?" I asked. I did not know it then nor was I to know it for quite a while, but the moment I lifted that telephone, my game was on its way to par.

"Your goal in golf," Lewis said, "is to play every hole in perfect par. The birdies will take care of themselves. Once you have a goal set up, your subconscious mind will tend to seek that goal." This is logical when you review it, since science now agrees that the subconscious mind is like a servo-mechanism. Once given a goal, it trains its radar beam on that goal like a homing torpedo on its target. In essence, this was the first suggestion Lewis gave me, and it was repeated about four times in the hypnotic state.

Then the suggestions were given to think and *hold on* to the thought "swing free and easy, relax, hit the ball, and par" before every game. It was at this juncture that my first technical improvement in golf became noticeable. The most obvious improvement was in my distance. For some reason, I ceased to scoop-slice my shots and began to hook the ball. I hooked my drives, my irons and my putts. The length of my drives increased 50 yards. Par-four holes that used to be attainable only with two-wood shots became a drive and seven-iron. My score dropped immediately to about 80. For a few weeks, while Lewis reinforced the idea of an easy swing, I kept hitting the ball better and better.

Then a new suggestion was given. It went like this: "Once your club is at the top of the swing and you are ready to swing into the ball, you mentally blank out on the downswing. The clubhead knows where to go; you leave the driving to your subconscious mind." For about a week after this suggestion, however, I played badly—in the middle 80's. At the end of a week, however, I began to hit the ball with less hook and more carry. I was a fair middle-iron and long-iron player, but my drives and short irons were getting better. At the same time my putting was getting worse. It seemed that the more greens I hit in par, the worse I would putt. One example of this was an 81 I shot that included 40 putts. At this point I believed that if my putting were to improve I could play at the par level.

We followed blank-out-on-the-swing with blank-out-on-the-backswing. When this suggestion had taken root, it was further suggested that once I thought of the phrase "relax, hit the ball," my body would automatically go into motion. This was further simplified into the phrase "one-two." The more simple the trigger mechanism can be made, the more efficiently it works.

One of the principal reasons behind every good golfer's success is the acquired or natural ability to concentrate a great deal of his conscious attention on the shot he is in the process of making. This concentration is not giving individual attention to a lot of little things but excluding all distractions such as opponents, weather and ego. This concentration allows the conscious mind to be momentarily penalty-free. When the ego or conscious mind is penalty-free, the muscles naturally feed back their duties to perform. The conscious mind or ego is then free to enjoy the pleasure of their performance. This is one of the important suggestions given to me by Lewis, not once but many, many times. This suggestion became more meaningful as time went by.

How does this sort of suggestion apply? In the late summer of 1966, I came to the ninth tee 3 under par. The ninth hole is 540 yards long. I teed up and drove the ball about 240 yards dead center. I was about 300 yards out from the green. Suddenly my ego said to me, "Swing hard to get near the green in 2 so you can get an easy shot at a birdie."

This is the wrong attitude because it imposes pressure. My thoughts should have been to get the easiest par possible, but I went for a birdie. I missed my three-wood shot and only hit it about 80 yards. Now I was in the impossible position of having to hit a well-trapped green from 220 yards out. This time, however, I forgot entirely about the missed shot. I was concentrating on hitting a correct three-wood shot.

My third shot was 30 feet from the hole, but I erased my effort by 3-putting from that point. My playing partner was Charlie Drouin, the man I mentioned earlier.

Later, I tried to analyze what had caused me to shoot an unbelievable 34 for nine. My 40 on the back nine, which we played first, gave me a 74 for the day, 1 over par! Never had I performed like this, and yet it was only the beginning. Every so often, say about one out of every three rounds I played for the rest of the season, I seemed to click. My goal now is to allow Lewis to train my mental faculties further so that I can shoot par most of the time.

Throughout my training periods with Lewis a tape recorder was used to reinforce and consolidate the gains already made. Once the muscles have received the initial correct training, they can only improve with practice, and let me make it clear that I spent a great deal of time hitting practice shots.

I must state here that at no time did either Lewis or myself concern ourselves with the physical aspects of golf. That is, we were not concerned with pivot, grip, stance, waggle or anything like that. We both assumed that these things were already in excellent working order. The car was there to be driven. All we did was put someone in the driver's seat.

IV. THE SHORT GAME

Most golfers, except for beginners and hopeless cases, can get reasonably close to the green on a par-four hole in three or four shots at the very worst. Yet these same golfers finish the round with all kinds of 6's, 7's and 8's on their card. The reason, of course, is that they take three, four and sometimes five strokes to put the ball into the cup from quite near the green. How many times have you heard someone grumble about taking a 7 after having been only 30 yards from the green in two shots? Obviously, then, the fastest way to lower your score is to stop wasting strokes around the green. It's all well and good to go to a driving range and hit bucket after bucket of balls with the woods, but some attention to pitching and chipping can also be rewarding. A little attention to the following advice should have the 7's and 8's disappearing from your card in no time.

The Automatic Punch Shot

by Harry Obitz and Dick Farley

When anyone discusses a good golf swing, he is usually referring to the better-than-average golfer—which means the fine amateur and the touring professional. For them, a big, full swing is not the dangerous proposition it is for the average golfer, who's mainly searching for control and consistency.

More than anything else, the average golfer just needs to find the fairways and greens a lot more often—and in a lot less strokes. Therefore, long arcs and full swings leave too much room for error and produce too many uncontrolled shots.

So for more precise swinging with almost automatic results, we suggest that the high handicapper (as well as anyone else who seeks more control on his shots) try the following method on for size. We think it will fit everyone and will show that what golfers everywhere have always been looking for is easily available with no readjustment of stance, ball position, basic grip or swing technique.

It might simply be called the automatic punch shot. Now this may sound too easy and too obvious, but it is often the obvious things that most readily escape notice. Simply put, the average amateur is a better judge of distance and a lot more accurate when he keeps his swing arc as short as possible. If you choke down on the club, the automatic shot will be just that—automatic. You won't have to make any conscious adjustment, because it will all come naturally.

The theory of choking down on the club works anywhere on the course. We'll start at the green and work backwards to the tee, since the putting stroke is the shortest and the method most visible. Now, the obvious result of choking down on the putter (as well as other clubs) is to bring everything closer together, hence cutting down the arc and the length of the backstroke or takeaway.

In addition, for short putts, choking down provides not only accuracy but a fine feel of the clubhead. With the decreased arc of the swing, the club naturally stays closer to the ground. And, since most golfers have never been told *how to hit firm putts,* this should automatically solve a

86

Choking down on the club, *left,* will automatically make your backswing shorter and will cause the weight to remain primarily on the left side. With this restricted body movement, you'll have more feel of the clubhead and therefore, get more accuracy on your iron shots.

large share of those three-putt greens and give you all the firmness necessary to getting down in two or less. However, to keep the club close to the ground on longer putts, you must use a longer club length. If you shorten up here, you'll probably chop down on the ball instead of hitting or stroking it.

When you get out to chipping range, say from 20 to 30 yards, this abbreviated method will keep the club on line and guarantee firmness through the shot. Any longer stroke invites that dangerous opening of the clubface and lifting the club on the takeaway.

Moving back once again brings us to the real need for control of the club and keeping the ball on line. From 50 to 120 yards, you might pick anything from an eight-iron to a pitching wedge, depending on how far from the pin and how strong you are. The purpose, of course, is to play a firm stroke instead of floating or lobbing the shot over the green or taking a mud-lifter halfway there.

The club and hand action on the punch shot, *left,* should be crisper and less sweeping than on a full iron shot. The clubhead will come into the ball at a sharper angle, providing lots of bite.

The technique of this choked-down punching action is really quite simple. The ball is played in exactly the same spot as usual. With the shortened grip, and thus the automatically shortened swing arc, about 70 percent of your weight will be kept on the left side, while normally the weight on the full shot is evenly distributed. This means that on the backswing, the club will naturally be drawn back on a sharper angle for a crisper and less sweeping return. The club action on the downswing is made primarily with the forearms and is a good deal more firm than on the fuller, longer-shafted swing.

Because distance is directly proportional to the number of inches you choke down on the club, it is vital to keep the following equation in mind: *Every inch you drop from the full length of the grip reduces the shot by 10 yards.* Since a golf club normally has 3 inches of length left after you've gripped it, those 3 inches are your control factor. Therefore, if you choke the club 3 inches down from the butt, 30 yards will be the maximum reduction on the shot. However, maximum reduction will give you maximum backspin.

If you shorten the grip on a pitching wedge (and hence the swing) to replace the distance lost or to achieve the same distance as you would get on the normal shot and grip, simply increase the speed of the clubhead coming into the ball. If you choke down even more, say 2 or 3 inches, you can't expect the same distance unless you go to a longer, less-lofted club. By choking down far enough (shortening the grip and therefore the swing), the seven-iron, for instance, can be reduced to the productive length of the wedge. Not only that, but it puts more spin or biting action on the ball.

When you come to the long irons and the woods, you can still choke down, remembering that the primary purpose is control of the club and the swing with consequent greater accuracy. On short par-fours especially, where there are more hazards per yard on the way to the green, control becomes increasingly vital. So, the normal 220–250 yards expected from a full drive is reduced to 200–210 yards, with the fairway now much more than just a shot in the dark. And it follows that the normal long-iron distance of 170–210 yards will drop back (with choking) to 140–180 yards—with greater precision.

To sum it all up then, the nature of this choked-down swing has the following *three automatic results:*

1. The sharper angle on the takeaway and downswing provides greater punching action and, therefore, greater bite. With a choked seven-iron, not only is there more control but, because of the greater abrasive action on the ball, there is more backspin than with a full nine-iron.
2. You are assured of more clubhead control because there is less tendency for the blade to haphazardly open or close.
3. The abbreviated swing means you're not going back too far or overswinging. It eliminates all that wrist-flipping at the shot or premature hitting from the top. On the return, you are forced to stay down, hit down and hit through the shot both easily and automatically.

Remember, the automatic punch shot involves no trick stance, no gimmicky cut shot or any other peculiar movement foreign to the good golf swing. It is natural, simple and eminently practical for the weekend golfer who wants to get out there and really score.

Chip to Save Par

by Pat Schwab

To save par on a green you've just missed, you must chip close enough for one putt. Whether the pin is only 15 feet away or as far as 90, the basic move is forward and down, with body rhythm and clubhead rhythm the same. This important shot calls for a two-point program: (1) pick a spot to hit to and (2) concentrate on how to execute it. Assuming you can read the green for roll and break, let's check out point two. Out of disappointment at being off target and the anxiety to make up for this error, the grip usually becomes too tight. So, *first,* you must ease up on your grip and hold the club as though you were holding a bag of feathers. You must be able to *feel* the clubhead in your fingers. *Second,* take the club back with a movement of the hands, arms and shoulders. The body otherwise remains firm, with the knees flexed to handle the slight weight shift without restriction. On the return to the ball, let the clubhead do the work, meaning the body and the clubhead must go through together. With practice, you'll send the ball repeatedly into one-putt territory.

The Soft Pitch

by Hank Davis III

Here's a shot that calls for a youngster's nerve, a veteran's poise and a champion's winning habit. It is named the "soft pitch" but it is a rather hard shot to master, because it is hit with a minimum of wrist break and body motion and it requires the fine touch of a well-stroked putt. From 20 to 100 feet out, a good wedge will produce best results. Move both the left and the right hand a bit to the left, into the weaker position. Hold the club lightly in the fingers of the right with a good, sensitive feel between the right forefinger and thumb. A little knock-kneed position will reduce the tendency to move the body. Play the ball off the left heel or just left of center from an open stance. Take the club slightly outside the line, with the left hand in the lead, slowly. Do not hurry the down-swing. You must wait for the club. The slow swing from beginning to end takes a lot of nerve and confidence. You have to rely on experience, poise and determination. The back of the left hand also starts the club down and continues its move on toward target. Keep the clubface square. By keeping the tempo of the swing constant, you can soon learn to control distance by length of backswing.

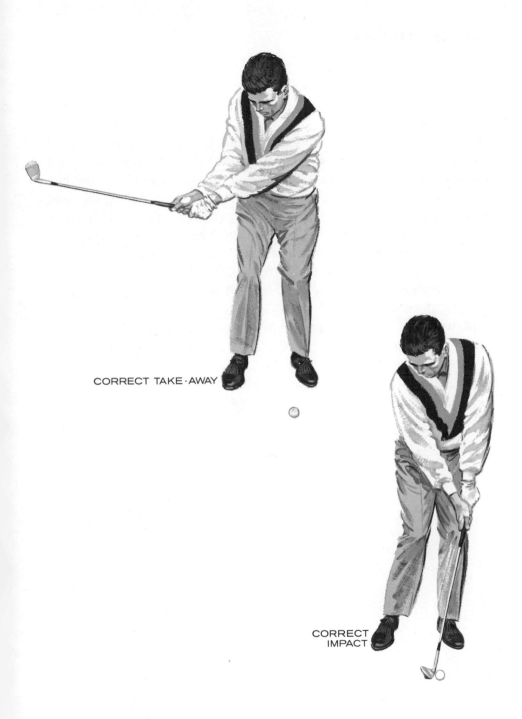

CORRECT TAKE-AWAY

CORRECT
IMPACT

93

One Bounce to the Pin

by Joe Redanty

The bump shot is a good short-distance shot because it will stop dead after the first bounce. It is not recommended or intended for great distances. To execute, take a half grip on the club and play the ball about center from a slightly open stance. Weight is on the left foot and remains there. In starting the backswing, pick the clubhead up more abruptly than with a normal short-iron shot. There is little shoulder and hip turn. The left heel stays tight to the turf. The main point of this bump shot is the action from the top of the swing, which is a half to three-quarter motion. The downswing is effected with the right knee quickly charging toward the ball. Success depends on the firmness of the left hand, wrist and arm at impact and just beyond impact. Notice that after impact a straight line is formed from the top of the left shoulder to the tip of the club. The trick is to keep the left wrist from collapsing at the hit.

Pitch and Run Attack

by Felice Torza

Picture a slight uphill situation in which the ball rests about 20 feet from the green and the cup is another 25 feet beyond. The pro will use a pitching wedge, matching his club to the estimated distance he figures the ball will roll after it lands from 3 to 6 feet beyond the edge of the green. The amateur will use the club he favors for playing pitch and run shots—probably a six- or seven-iron.

No.6 OR No.7 IRON (INCORRECT)

Picture the same situation but with the cup 50 feet from the edge of the green. The pro will use a six-iron here, again figuring to land the ball 3 to 6 feet inside the green and running it approximately 45 feet. The six-iron gives the necessary low trajectory making the ball run this far. The amateur, too, in this case will use the correct club—a six- or seven-iron—not by design but from habit.

No.6 OR No.7 IRON (CORRECT)

Now envision a third situation in which the ball rests about 20 feet from a downhill green, with the cup 50 feet in. The pitching wedge or nine-iron should be used here, again landing the ball from 3 to 6 feet inside the edge of the green. It will run the remaining 45 feet or so of its own momentum. Use a six- or seven-iron, though, and the ball will probably run off the other side of the green.

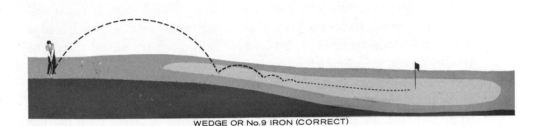

WEDGE OR No.9 IRON (CORRECT)

The Pitch and Run Shot

by Elmer Voight

In the golfing repertoire the pitch and run, or "drag" shot, is indispensable. It is made from anywhere inside 50 yards with a punch-wedge down to a seven- or six-iron. Basically, this is a left backhand shot. The weight should be completely on your left foot, hands in front of the clubhead, and feet fairly close together—about 4 to 7 inches apart. Hood the blade, making, for instance, a nine-iron into the loft of a seven-iron, and take the club back low and square to the target with the left hand. *Do not transfer the weight to the right side.* Keeping the clubface square to the target throughout, remain as quiet as you can in the execution and let the short follow-through be stopped naturally by the weight held on the left side and the lack of body action or turn. The ball will land running—like a putt. Note: *The right hand should never lead the left.* As a mental guide to "getting the touch," try to imagine how hard you would strike the ball if you held a putter in your hand from the same distance. Practice will guarantee success (and profit) around the greens with this quiet iron surgery.

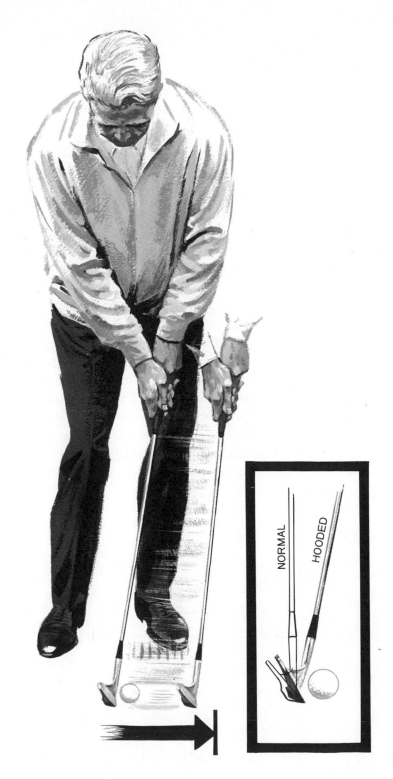

NORMAL

HOODED

99

Don't Waste It, Bank It

by Dick Masterson

I believe that most golfers overuse the pitching wedge without considering the type of lie they have or the kind of shot required. The average golfer is usually somewhere short as well as to the right or left of the green. Most greens are also banked on the sides, and a pin placement tucked in close to the edge with traps nearby increases the difficulty of a good wedge execution. Heavy traffic of carts and golf shoes from 30 to 40 yards in results in much hard-pan and a wedge here becomes both dangerous and costly. First, the wedge may bounce off the hard-pan and either sail the ball over the green or skull it into a trap. Second, with a tight lie and a close-cut pin, only a superwedge will be adequate. To save a stroke, take advantage of the terrain by rolling the ball up the bank, or, preferably, chipping it into the bank and bouncing the ball up onto the green. For this you need a straighter-faced club—a seven-, six- or five-iron. With the longer shafts, choke down somewhat, stand near the ball with your arms and hands close to your body, feet together, weight on the left side, and the ball centered (or slightly back farther) in your stance. You'll find that greater success is yours in a running shot rather than a doubtful wedge.

Tracking the Seven-Iron

by Herb Thienell

If you want to hit the seven-iron straight to the flagstick, don't take the club straight back from the ball. Instead, *take it back a little inside the line* so you'll be in the groove to return the club on the same path. Most golfers realize the need for a straight ball, but, for some reason, as soon as they get within seven-iron distance of the green, they try to steer the ball. The next time you are within 135–150 yards of your target, envision two straight lines or "railroad tracks" pointing in the direction of flight, as illustrated. The stance line serves to guide your feet into a slightly open position by drawing the left foot back; the other line running through the ball is to guide the club into an inside-out swing. Once set, take the club back low but inside the line, make a full shoulder turn and get your hands up around shoulder level. You're now ready to lash into the ball, arching it toward the green with proper loft and backspin to make it hit on line and bite.

Don't Stiff-arm the Shot

by Tony Kaczenski

On the 10- to 20-yard chip shot, club selection depends on what you want to do with the ball, where you want it to land, how much control you need and the contour of the green. I use anything from an eight-iron to a pitching wedge, because these clubs get the ball up faster. The general approach to the chip is an open stance, which keeps the body from interfering with the proper hand and arm movement, and the ball is played off the left foot to take advantage of the loft of the club. The club must be taken back far enough so that you *don't stiff-arm the shot,* and on the return, for good control, the *left hand must lead*. Letting the right hand take over will always spell disaster. And, lastly, concentrate on the actual hit. The amateur usually lifts his eyes off the ball—and then scuffs or tops it. So watch the clubhead meet the ball.

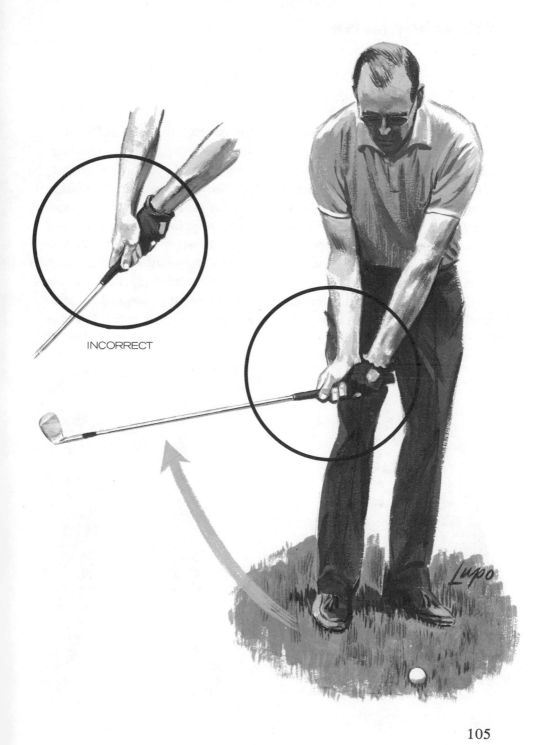

INCORRECT

Chip the Way You Putt

by Herb Wimberly

The old adage "Drive for show, putt for dough" could be enlarged to include the short chip-and-run, a phase of the game that causes considerable woe to many golfers. This shot, from just off the putting surface, can be terribly inconsistent when a player tries to make a drastic change from a successful putting style. Using a six-iron, *execute the pitch-and-run just as if you were putting.* This includes gripping the club with your putting grip and, most important, *choking down to a point that will equal the putter length.* Swing tempo, weight distribution, ball position in the stance and even preparatory steps to the actual execution should compare with your putting technique. More one-putt greens and an occasional chip-in will result from this adjustment to the short game. If you're a reasonably good putter, there's no reason you shouldn't be just as accurate with the short chip.

106

Why the Short Irons?

by Roger Ganem

The original niblick, the old trouble shooter whose counterpart is today's nine-iron, was designed for the express purpose of hacking the ball out of heavy grass which bordered most of the fairways of the links of yesteryear, or out of cart tracks, or other awkward places. The condition of those courses was such that the extrication of the ball was accompanied by a most powerful effort on the part of the golfer. The awesome result was usually a large displacement of real estate, a sprained wrist or two, and a cry of "Forc," often followed by a count of five, six and seven.

It is little wonder that one humorous soul named his niblick "Faith" because, as he explained it, faith can move mountains.

Today, thanks to golf courses more carefully groomed and implements more scientifically made, there's more reason for hope than need for faith, and accuracy with the short irons is something even the high handicap golfers have come to expect.

Much of this confidence in hitting shots to the pin from within 140 yards with seven-, eight-, nine-irons and the pitching and sand wedges is a result of continued improvement in golf-club design. Now we do not wish to take anything away from the steady increase in personal proficiency and the efforts of the teaching professionals, but the clubs must come in for their share of the credit.

As the clubs in your set get shorter in length, they also get heavier, and this extra weight is placed in the blade, usually directly behind the point of impact. The wider head and the thicker sole are also aids since the golfer is generally flying the ball with his short irons and, the shot is higher because of the extra loft. He wants to get some backspin and gets it because of the fine weight distribution and the lower point of impact.

Next, to control the heavier blade so that it doesn't twist away from being square to the target, the makers shorten the distance between the last "step" on the shaft and the top of the hosel. This reduction in distance makes for a stiffer shaft, and a stiff shaft is easier to control than one that is flexible. Thirdly, they unerringly have fitted the shaft to the blade so that the center line of the shaft is directed precisely at the point of impact, and what better sighting device can a player have? All together, this means the player is using a precision instrument with which he can pinpoint his approach shot. These built-in advantages give the modern golfer an edge when he's using any of the short irons, aptly called the pay-off clubs.

The short irons are the seven-iron, which measures $36\frac{7}{16}''$ in length, has a 39-degree loft and a normal lie of $60\frac{1}{2}$ degrees; the eight-iron, 36, 43 and $61\frac{1}{4}$ respectively; the nine-iron, $35\frac{9}{16}$, 47 and 62: the pitching wedge, $34\frac{5}{8}$, 54 and $63\frac{1}{4}$; and the sand wedge, $34\frac{5}{8}$, 58 and 63. The all-purpose wedge, which is not recommended because it is neither fish nor fowl, measures $34\frac{5}{8}$, 55 and 63 respectively. Bear in mind that these specifications are general, and they may vary among manufacturers, but the variance will be slight.

The loft of a club is the angle of the clubface, and the experts who play for pay feel this style gets the club under and through the ball with no loss in tempo or direction.

A difference in blade design also exists in the wedges. Some have an *inverted* bottom line, which, when the club is held straight down, features a leading edge that is *higher than the flange in back*. This is the famous "bouncer" club, ideal for those who like to bounce the ball out of traps by hitting the sand one to two inches behind the ball. The flange in the back makes contact with the sand before the leading edge does and prevents the club from becoming embedded in the sand. The club continues under and through the ball, without interruption, and the ball pops out of the sand as nice as you please. The opposing stylist prefers a square blade because he would rather "slide" the ball out. With this club, the sand is hit about the same distance behind the ball, but the action of the club, not the ball, differs slightly.

The wedge, as you undoubtedly know, was developed by Gene Sarazen, and many feel that it is responsible for the phenomenal scoring of the modern professionals and the top-flight amateur players. But it is also responsible for many truly bad shots, most of them from the fairway.

Shots that are missed from sand traps might be the result of fear or panic, and the club would not be the culprit. But when the player stubbornly tries to use the sand wedge from the fairway, especially the one with the inverted bottom line and the heavy flange, and the club bounces instead of getting under and through, the result is a skulled shot. If you use a sand wedge from the fairway be sure to keep your hands ahead so as to allow the leading edge of the clubhead to come into the shot first.

The thing to do about cutting your strokes instead of the ball, the manufacturers say, is to have both wedges, and in this respect they may not be trying to sell a bill of goods. Just keep in mind that the Rules do not permit you to carry more than 14 clubs in your bag. The runner-up in the 1965 U.S. Amateur, by one shot, was penalized four strokes just for this reason.

The fear of hitting into the belly of the ball and ruining both the shot and the ball is a hand-me-down that dates back to the feather-ball period prior to 1848. The featheries were leather-covered balls stuffed with boiled goose feathers, stitched up securely, hammered hard and round and given three coats of paint. They were rather difficult to make; at best, ball makers were able to turn out only about four a day.

In wet weather, they tended to become sodden and would fly apart. Even in good weather, a misdirected shot with an iron club might spell the end of the game for the unlucky player, who otherwise would have been fortunate if his featherie lasted through two rounds. So it was that the original niblicks were said to have been wooden clubs, sometimes called the fifth "spoon."

The one club that was used for the high pitch shot over a hazard and onto the green was the baffing spoon. With this club the masters of that era obtained backspin by "baffing" or striking the ground with the flat sole of the club a fraction of a second before impact with the ball, which was caught by the club as it rebounded off the turf. How is that for finesse? Of course, they used an open stance.

The first iron niblicks were short in blade, designed solely to get the golf balls out of the cart ruts made by the horse-drawn wagons which were allowed to travel the roads on the early town-owned courses. These clubs were appropriately called track or rut irons and measured a mere 2 inches or so in diameter. Some were smaller.

In comparison, today's nine-iron, measuring about 2 by 3 inches in the hitting area, seems large. But the size of the blade just didn't gradually increase from the track-iron size to its present size. One of the most unique niblicks was the one used by the winner of the 1883 British

Open, Willie Fernie. The blade of his trouble club measured no less than 3½ by 4½ inches. However, the iron was almost wafer thin. Still, it would be legal today.

On the other hand, the club with the deeply slotted face used by Jock Hutchison in winning the British Open in 1921 was immediately banned and it, as well as any like it, remains illegal to this day.

The amount and depth of the face scoring (lines on the blade) of the iron clubs are specified (not standardized) in Rule 2-2d, and in the Note to this Rule, of the USGA Rules of Golf. So the miracles of precision shooting by the top touring professionals are being performed with the very same clubs you can purchase at your pro shop.

The clubs used by Willie Fernie, Jock Hutchison and other champions of the world's major tournaments are on exhibit at the USGA Golf House in New York.

V. THE SAND TRAP

Without a doubt, the single most frightening shot the average golfer faces is one from a greenside sand trap. Invariably, because of this fear, he either jams his club into the ground, leaving the ball in the trap, or hits the ball flush and knocks it far over the green. The shot, however, not only shouldn't cause terror, it should be regarded as relatively easy—because it is. Many pros, in fact, often prefer going into a trap to playing from thick grass behind the green. The pros themselves don't always get down in two shots from a trap, but they often do, and what's more important, they always get the ball out and put it somewhere on the green. It isn't all that difficult, and by reading the following pages closely, you should soon be playing those sand shots with confidence.

The ABC's of the Sand Shot

by Harry Obitz and Dick Farley

There is one main objective in sand play—get out. In order to do this, every golfer should understand first how to play the basic shot—often called the explosion shot.

Too many players get confused by advice to "close the blade a little on this lie" or "open it up on that." They are forever trying to make the ball do "tricks" every time they step into a greenside bunker. In ninety cases out of one hundred, all that is called for is a straightforward, regular explosion shot.

That's why we'll discuss here the variations on the basic trap shot. Having built on this foundation, we can deal at a later date with those "tough" lies and different sand textures that demand changes from the normal technique.

Until you gain a lot of experience and confidence in your trap play, it's easiest to use a three-quarter swing as your standard stroke. You can then vary the distance the ball travels by making the club enter the sand two inches, one inch, or half an inch behind the ball. To make the ball go the maximum distance, you would take the ball first, then a divot of sand, in the same way as you would hit an iron shot from the fairway.

Most trap shots are missed because the golfer has no clear idea as to how to play them. First, perhaps, he'll try to "flick" it clean off the top of the sand with his wrists, only to have the ball catch the lip of the trap and roll down to his feet again.

For his second try, perhaps he will take a wild, full slash that results in the club being buried four or five inches behind the ball, which goes all of a couple of feet. Need we go on? These golfers treat the sand as their enemy although, in fact, it is the medium through which they can control the length and trajectory of the shot.

Many golfers also don't appreciate how well-designed the sand wedge is for its job. Compared to a nine-iron it has more weight, more loft and a much wider flange. It also is appreciably deeper from the top to the bottom of the face.

The sand iron's extra weight enables it to cope more easily with the sand's resistance. Its extra loft makes it easier for the golfer to get the ball up and out of the trap. The wide flange makes it skid rather than dig deep into the sand and stop. And its extra depth from the top to the bottom of the face gives a good safety margin for making contact with the ball.

To illustrate the merits of a sand wedge, let's take the case where you're trapped around 10–15 yards from the pin. The ball is lying fair, with no more than a quarter of its surface beneath the sand. The sand is of average texture—not hard or wet, nor extra-soft and fluffy. Here's how you play the shot:

Take a slightly open stance, as on any other short iron shot, with the left foot withdrawn a little from the line of flight. The ball should be off the left heel. Keep the stance narrow, with your heels not more than six inches apart. A narrow stance keeps you "over the ball" to deliver a precision blow. If the stance were wider, you well might sway to the right on the backswing. As a result you would hit too far behind the ball on the downswing to be effective.

As on every other shot, the right foot is at right angles to the line. The left foot is turned 45 degrees toward the hole in order to enable the body to make a full forward pivot, forcing the club to a complete finish.

On this 10–15 yard shot, aim to enter the sand 2 inches behind the ball. Address the ball with the clubface square to the line, that is with the line of the leading edge at right angles to the line of flight.

Your swing naturally will be on a more upright plane than for any other club because the sand wedge has the shortest shaft of all the irons and this dictates that the ball be played closer to the feet than on any other shot. The arms and hands should be close to the body at address with very little daylight showing between the body and the hands.

The "feel" of the swing is that it is more "straight up and down" than for any other shot, but this is due entirely to the naturally very upright action with a short-shafted and extra-heavy club. Emphasizing the "cocking" or bending of the right arm on the backswing will help you get the right action.

The tempo of the swing should be a little more leisurely than on a nine-iron pitch. This in turn dictates that the backswing will be of sufficient length to keep the entire stroke smooth. Remember, no stabbing at the ball, or chopping. Your backswing should be around three-quarters of what you normally make on a full shot.

In the standard trap shot, the ball is played off the left heel at address, with the stance open and the heels no more than six inches apart. The right foot is at a right angle to the line of flight and the left foot is turned out at a 45-degree angle. The hands and arms are close to the body. The right arm cocks early, and by the top of the swing, the left knee has moved forward and the weight shifted to the right foot. The right side, from hip to shoulder, has been drawn back while the cocking of the right arm has carried the club up in an upright plane to the correct

position. On the downswing, the left hip pulls back as the right knee goes forward, shifting the weight back to the left foot. The downswing is dominated by the stretching of the left side, an action that contracts the left arm and pulls the club down into the hitting area. The right arm exerts the power that was stored in it by correct cocking on the backswing, then straightens out to apply the club-head to the ball and continue the stroke to a smooth, balanced finish.

The stroke must be completed with a full follow-through. With all the best trap players—exceptionally fine examples are Julie Boros and Sam Snead—most of the action *appears* to take place from the moment the clubhead enters the sand until the full, free finish of the swing. Although this is an illusion, nevertheless it is an indication of the importance of completing the shot.

The club must pass through the ball on all normal trap shots to keep the ball on line, and assure getting it out of the trap. The sand wedge stroke must be definitely thought of as a *cutting* action into the sand, under and through the ball. The cutting action, combined with the angle of the clubface as it passes through the impact area and the amount of sand taken, produces the various spins and trajectories vital to ball control from the trap.

Now let's examine in a little more detail what happens to the club and ball in the impact area.

When the wedge enters the sand 2 inches behind the ball, the clubhead passes *under* the ball, with a cushion of sand about ¾ of an inch thick between clubface and ball.

Because the club flange is about ¾ of an inch below the ball, the striking force of the club will have to come from the top portion of the blade. The heavy weight of the club flange at impact is *underneath* rather than behind the ball—as with a sand iron shot off the fairway. This gives a higher trajectory to the shot than normal.

The large amount of sand between the clubface and the ball prevents the grooves on the face from gripping the ball. This means there will be little or no backspin—the ball will come out softly and fall like a feather on the green, rolling very little.

The result, therefore, of using the standard sand iron swing and hitting 2 inches behind the ball is maximum height and minimum backspin.

Using the same stance and swing formula the golfer can add an additional 5 yards to the carry by simply entering the sand 1 inch instead of 2 inches behind the ball.

As the club comes in to the sand 1 inch closer to the ball, it is not below the ball as much as before. This means that the ball will be struck a little lower on the face of the club and that the weight of the flange will not be so far underneath the ball as in the first case. Therefore, the trajectory will not be quite as high as when the club enters the sand 2 inches behind the ball.

Hitting 1 inch behind the ball will now impart some backspin, because there is now less sand between the face and the ball. However, it will not give as much backspin as when the club strikes still closer to the ball.

An interesting thing happens when you strike ½ inch behind the ball in the sand with the standard three-quarter stroke. This application of the clubface will find a very thin layer of sand between the face and the ball. You will notice it increases the abrasive action of the clubface on the ball, producing maximum backspin. This is how the experts make the ball bite and jump back from its landing point on the green.

Hitting ½ inch behind the ball also means that most of the flange weight strikes on the *back of the ball* rather than below it as in the case of the shots already discussed. The weight coming in on the back of the ball will drive it forward on a lower trajectory and for a greater distance.

To produce the maximum distance and the lowest trajectory, the ball should be contacted first and then the sand. Here the backspin is caused by the ball simply being squeezed between the clubface and the sand, much in the same fashion as in a normal iron shot off the turf. A good amount of stop can be expected from this shot—although not quite as much as when you enter the sand ½ inch behind the ball and have the extra backspin caused by the abrasive action of the sand.

The trajectory of the shot is, of course, the lowest of the four shots we've described, because the weight of the flange strikes on the back of the ball, more so even than in the case of the "½-inch behind" shot.

Note that we haven't said a word about changing the standard three-quarter length swing. This is quite deliberate, as the only change necessary to send the ball the desired height and length is the different distance you hit behind the ball.

Our formula for this can be expressed quite simply: The farther behind the ball you enter the sand, the more height, the less backspin and the less distance; the closer you hit to the ball, the less height, the more backspin and the greater distance. It's as easy as that.

No discussion of trap play would be complete without stressing the power of positive thinking—an overworked phrase, perhaps, but like many such sayings it has been overworked precisely because it is true.

The next time you get into a trap, take your stance for your standard trap shot and calculate how far behind the ball you should strike into the sand. Tell yourself you will execute a full, smooth three-quarter swing. You also should have positive thoughts of holing the shot. If you think merely of "getting out," you will seldom put the ball within holeable distance.

Whatever you do, don't get fancy next time you are in a trap. Your standard explosion shot will put you near the hole from all but the toughest lies.

It's Not as Tricky as It Looks

by Kyle Burton

One of the more difficult shots in golf is the 30- to 50-yard bunker shot. And I must say that most golfers scare themselves into missing this shot even before hitting the ball. First, discard the sand wedge, as it's too difficult to control from this distance. Use an eight- or nine-iron. *Actually, it is played like a pitch-and-run, from a square stance with the feet not more than a foot apart. The ball is positioned off the right foot and the hands remain ahead of the clubblade all the way through the shot. At no time should the clubface open. It is important that the clubhead contact the ball and the sand at the same time.* If you hit the ball first, you won't get it over the lip of the bunker, and if you hit the sand first, you might leave the ball in the sand. *You must keep your head still and never take your eyes off the ball.* The clubhead is driven down through the ball and into the sand. Your follow-through will be naturally shorter than normal. *Remember, this is no explosion, or cut shot. You must keep the face of the club slightly closed and the hands leading at all times.* Never open the clubface on the backswing, and work on moving the head of the club well through the ball.

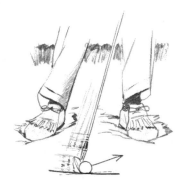

Popping the Ball from Sand

by Buck Worsham

When bunkered, have you been leaving the ball in the sand, instead of popping it out near the pin? Then try these tips: (1) Look at the back of the ball instead of one or two inches behind it. (2) Position the clubhead slightly inside the ball, toward the body, instead of flush center. It is my observation that the average player who looks at a target behind the ball flinches and hits two or three inches farther back than he intends to hit. The result is that he leaves the ball in the trap. As for positioning the club slightly inside the ball, the general tendency is to swing on a line outside that of the address position, and the ball will be struck with the neck (hosel) of the club. For the sand shot, then, use the slightly open stance and keep the hands a bit behind the ball to let the flange come into play. The ball is positioned in line with the left arch. If the ball is sitting clean, open the clubface; if buried, close the face. On a severe uphill stance, play the ball off the left foot; on a severe downhill stance, play it off the right foot. For easy remembering—always play the ball off the high foot, whether you are in a trap or on the fairway.

Don't Slug—Slide

by Lew Worsham

The term "blast shot" is basically a poor expression. It implies *slugging* and suggests brute strength instead of finesse. The right idea is one of slapping or flipping the ball out of the bunker. The large flange is designed to prevent the clubhead from digging in and coming to a sudden halt. First, to get this feeling of sliding through the sand, take a few swings on some firm turf. Open the face of the club and with a rather loose grip try to take a small divot. You'll find the flange will almost bounce off the ground. This is the action you need in the sand. Second, when most players are asked what they should look at when "trap-shooting," their answer inevitably is *the ball*. This is fine from the fairway, but it doesn't follow that in the sand you should look at the ball and yet hit somewhere else. That's how you leave it in the sand and lose strokes. The eyes should be focused on a definite spot behind the ball. To fix this notion in the mind, place a ball on a level lie in the trap and, with your fingers, draw a line about a foot long and two inches behind the ball. *This is the spot at which you should look.*

TURF TRIAL

Outside-Inside Sand Shot

by Jimmy Wright

Of the many ways to hit a sand shot, a good number are useless. A too-low backswing and you'll hit too far behind the ball; swing with a left-hand lead and the club stays open at impact while the blade slices under the ball; sway with the club in either direction and you'll take too much sand or too much ball. To guard against all this, from an open stance, *your first move off the ball should be a sharp wrist break*. This takes the club up and back *outside the line. Next make a good shoulder turn so the club moves to the inside.* This keeps you over the ball and in position to make the shot. As soon as you start the downswing, it becomes a *hit with the right hand,* forcing the clubface to make a track through the sand and pointing to the intended line, rather than one that goes from the outside in or to the left. The blade that was open at address squares itself as soon as the right hand takes over, and the ball comes up and out and on target. So, practice hitting in the sand (without the ball) and if you can move the sand out, you can move the ball out, too. The right hand coming into play makes this shot much easier and puts you consistently in the right groove.

Chip from the Trap

by Stan Karman

This is a golfing era when the wedge is generally regarded as the "do-all" around the greens, and yet I feel that the average golfer who doesn't play too much would do much better chipping from a trap with a shallow-faced club. You can play it with a seven-, eight- or nine-iron, depending on the lie and how much green you have to work with, and it will pay off in more accuracy and control. Position the ball in line with the left instep and the hands forward. Use an open stance with the weight on the left foot. What you must do is *hit the ball before striking the sand*. The clubface is kept straight and the *right hand punches through* to keep from hitting behind the ball and stopping. It is a one-piece, hands, arms and shoulder shot made with a steady tempo and struck just a *fraction harder than if you were chipping from grass*. It's a real stroke-saver, particularly if you're one of the many players who has a terror of exploding clear over the green.

HANDS AHEAD

WEIGHT ON
LEFT FOOT

OPEN STANCE

Lupo

BALL OFF LEFT INSTEP

HIT BALL FIRST

The Sand in That Trap

The encyclopedias define sand as "any earth material that consists of loose grains of minerals or rocks larger than silt but smaller than gravel" and the dictionary describes it as a "loose granular material resulting from the disintegration of rocks." But there are more types of sand than there are definitions, and almost any kind may be in that sand trap.

Every state in the Union is a producer of sand. The varieties are so widespread and mingled that it is impossible to say that any one type is endemic to a specific region. For example, in Texas, sand found near Houston is usually brown and extremely fine, but San Antonio sand is perfectly white, more coarse, and ideal for sand traps. California sand can vary from a volcanic, rocky substance to the dazzlingly white stuff of the Monterey Peninsula that is as fine as powdered sugar. To confuse the matter further, golf architects seldom construct traps out of the sand found in the area because most sand is unsuitable for traps—it is too coarse or too fine, too full of clay or too rocky. The sand in the traps of the Augusta National course comes from South Carolina, not Georgia, and the traps on most courses are filled with imported sand.

The kind of sand in a trap critically affects the type of shot that must be made. This is because of the two basic principles of the explosion shot: (1) The clubhead never touches the ball. (2) Varying the shot requires that the golfer make an adjustment either in the distance behind the ball that the club strikes, or in the power of the swing, or a combination of both. Golf teachers have inculcated the mechanics of the simple explosion so thoroughly that even the beginner should know them, but unless he is aware of these two underlying principles, he will not be able to adjust to the varying resistances of sand used in traps.

The rules of golf forbid testing the sand with your hands or any part of the club. You must try to judge the texture and depth as you assume your stance, digging in, wiggling and fidgeting with your feet to learn all you can.

Dry, powdery, deep, fine and *artificial silicon* sands are usually the toughest to get out of. In extremely fine sand, the ball tends to bury itself in its own depression. The player should hit a spot about an inch behind the ball, and it will help to close the blade of the wedge so that the flange will not bounce and keep the clubhead from digging deep. Even hooding the face of the club will not prevent the clubhead's tendency to lose much of its speed as it ploughs through the heavy sand, so the golfer should concentrate on not quitting on the shot. Because so much sand gets between the face of the club and the ball, it is almost impossible to produce backspin on this full explosion shot, so expect your ball to roll a good bit after it hits the green. Surprisingly, you will have to dig your feet very deep in order to get a firm stance in a powdery trap, because although you slide into small-grained sand very easily, the stance is slippery and not secure. All of these tips apply even more strongly to the ersatz sand made of silicon compounds. It is finer than the most powdery real sand.

In *coarse, wet* or *shallow* sand, the best shot is usually the half-explosion. Very coarse and well-soaked sand is like a cushion below the ball—a cushion that will resist the clubhead and may make the flange of the wedge bounce up and into the ball. To avoid this tendency to skull the shot, hit about three inches behind the ball. You will get more distance out of wet or coarse sand, but because there is less sand between the ball and the clubface, you will get more backspin, too. In the gravelly sand that is sometimes found in New England, the ball will sit up nicely, and you may be able to play a chip from the trap; in any case it will be easy to produce backspin. The dirty, clotted, compacted sand that is sometimes found in the Southwest is most conducive to the half-explosion. In very shallow traps, where there is only a thin layer of sand on top of a hard base, play a very soft explosion so that the club will not dig too deeply and strike the base. Two bits of advice on wet sand: (1) When you assume your stance, check to see whether the sand is wet below the top skin—it may be dry two inches down, and this can make the shot play more like one from dry sand. (2) If there is no lip on the bunker, you may be able to putt out of drenched sand.

In any case, there is only one way to improve your skill in all kinds of sand. Once upon a time, a spectator was watching Jerry Barber practice his sand play. Shot after shot rolled up to within a few inches of the hole, until finally the inevitable happened and one ball went in. The man laughed, turned to Barber and said, "Jerry, you sure are lucky out of the sand." Barber smiled and replied, "Yes, and the more I practice, the luckier I get."

And so will you.

No More Terror in the Trap

by Jim Turnesa

Climb into a bunker with almost any average golfer and you'll find the dominant emotion will be fear. With all the sure-fire, foolproof equipment, the trap shot, strangely enough, still remains the most dreaded in golf.

Of course, I can't really talk about the average golfer because there is no such thing as the average golfer. There are only individual golfers with individual problems—and individual swings. Yet, we can suggest certain methods that have proved themselves successful for a large number of golfers and, therefore, worth mentioning, remembering and using. The practical advantage in these methods lies in lowering the golfer's score. And what golfer finding himself trapped in the sand can ignore such aid? What prisoner would refuse his freedom?

Although most sand traps are situated around the green, golfers do occasionally in a day's round land in fairway traps, so that's where we'll start.

In general, to take a wood from a fairway trap is to take a risky club at a most difficult time. If the sand has a hard surface, it may be a fine idea, but if the sand is soft and loose, the odds are that the wood will sink in and plow up sand in front of the clubface. The result is a "puff" shot or a smothered ball. And even if you have a good lie, you can't ignore the lip of the trap, especially since the ball usually flies out of the sand a little lower than normally. That makes two good reasons for taking a club with more loft than you would usually use from the same distance in the fairway. All of which means that you should select an iron, not a wood. A third and final reason for using a lofted iron like a five, six or seven, is that *the whole object here is to get the next one on the green, not the first one*.

Although it would be nice to get all the distance possible from whatever club you choose, to take a wild, violent lurch at the ball is not only pointless but ineffective. Swing naturally, but choke down on the club and restrict your backswing to a shorter arc for greater control and balance. Once you've gained solid footing, keep your weight on the left side more than on the right—it's even advisable to stand somewhat flat-footed—and contact the sand last, the ball first, hitting down and through, just as you do with an iron from the fairway.

And don't forget, never be overambitious on your club selection. Always play it safe from a fairway trap, taking one less club for the shot than you need. However, you can take one more than you need if the lip is not in your way.

Now we come to the sand shot around the green. And it is my feeling that any time you dump the ball in the bunker, you have an automatic club to come to the rescue—the sand wedge—and an automatic shot—the blast! There's no need to make it harder on yourself by hesitating over a seven-, eight-, nine-iron or pitching wedge. Use the one tool designed for the job.

However, anyone who can escape from the sand with a weapon other than a sand wedge has got to be right in his club selection. Who's to say he's wrong if he gets it out? For example, if you're successful with a seven-iron or a pitching wedge, I won't insist you must play the shot my way. If you get out consistently, you must be right. But, none the less, the odds favor those who have a standard approach to the trap shot that does not require an unusual method. And, I say again, the percentages are on the side of those who blast rather than those who chip out. And yet, as a matter of fact, during a tournament in Tacoma, Washington, my ball found a greenside trap that had no lip, so I used a putter and put it a few inches from the cup. Therefore, in a final choice between blasting or chipping out, between an iron or a wedge, you must use your best judgment.

Assuming you take a sand wedge into the trap, there are four cautionary ground rules to observe:

(1) Don't change your basic grip.
(2) Don't change your basic swing pattern.
(3) Don't swing too hard or overswing.
(4) Don't take a lot of sand.

In other words, no matter what kind of sand shot you face, the basic style of play remains the same. Minor adjustments may occur on uphill,

1

2

For any uphill lie in the sand, the key is to hit up and not into the bank itself, where the club will be buried. However, since the ball will jump higher with the

5

6

132

open clubface angled back, and since you will naturally take more sand with this shot, swing a little harder than normally.

On a downhill lie, since you're forbidden to touch the sand on the backswing, simply take the club back more steeply and follow through to a full finish. Failure

5

6

to do so will leave the club buried in the sand—and the ball as well. And, just like on the fairway, the ball is played off the highest foot—in this case, the right.

downhill, sidehill or lip lies, but the swing essentially is the same one you used on the tee and in the fairway.

Once you take an open stance with your feet wedged into the sand for balance, comfort and firm footing, you place the clubface in an open position above and behind the ball. (Grounding the club in the sand costs a stroke penalty.) This open blade at address does not require any grip change but merely a turning of your hands (which have already gripped the club properly) to the right. And keep the blade open all the way through the swing, going back and coming down. Note: On no trap shot is the blade closed.

Now, since the trap shot is mostly an arm swing, the hands are not as involved in execution as on other shots. If the hands do anything during the swing, they help push the club back to give you full extension of the arms and a high upright arc. And, on the return, the left arm will lead through the shot, throwing the open blade out toward the flag and the ball up and out toward the hole. At all costs, avoid trying to flip, scoop or shovel the ball out with a lot of wasted hand action.

The keys then to this basic bunker shot are an open blade throughout, a deliberate point of entry into the sand behind the ball, a definite follow-through and, above all, a slow and rhythmical swing. This is a comparatively effortless stroke, and no attempt should be made to rush it. The object should always be to take a fairly shallow divot of sand from underneath the ball, without the blade of the club actually touching the ball. And finally, if you want a good mental picture of what a good trap shot looks like, try to imagine the ball rolling up and off the face of the club as you come into the ball.

The few minor changes from this basic method are swinging harder and/or swinging deeper. For instance, to get added distance merely swing a little harder—that's all. From a buried lie just hit a little more deeply, keeping the same steady tempo and basic swing. Don't rush it and don't do anything drastic or extraordinary. As far as wet and dry sand are concerned, there's really not too much difference when you come right down to it except that in wet sand the ball comes out more easily because the club will not dig in.

How hard should you swing? Well, as a helpful gauge, I would say that the swing for the pitching wedge at 60 feet is approximately the same as a sand wedge from a trap at 40 feet. And you should use this sort of ratio in judging all blast shots.

Actually, you don't have to hit very hard at all, but *you do have to hit near the ball*. Which means you don't need a lot of sand. A minimum will do, say, an inch to a half inch, or even less. Usually the golfer misunderstands this instruction and takes too much. If the teacher says take an inch or two, the student goes ahead and hits too far behind, taking four to six inches, which is plainly much too much.

Directly related to this taking of sand is the golfer's notion that the one sure clue to surviving all trap shots is knowing what to fix his eyes on. To be perfectly frank, you don't have to stare at any special spot or stone, dimple on the ball or crease in the sand. Rather, you should be thinking of the whole swing; not how close to the ball you should hit or how hard you should strike the sand. Once you're set and know what you want to do, it's the whole swing that produces the shot, and not any one isolated piece of it.

And since no shot can be mastered without practice, go out to your golf course in the evenings, when there is still enough light to see what you're doing, and drop a dozen balls in a trap. Place them in various lies and then put into practice the things you've just read. Once you know you can get out, you will.

VI. PUTTING

There is no single correct way to putt. The best teachers will offer advice on certain basic things every golfer should do, but even they admit that, in the final analysis, putting is a matter of feel. If it were all that easy, you wouldn't see the stars of the professional tour experimenting with different putters and a variety of grips. However, after you have arrived at a stance that suits you and have practiced enough to acquire a good touch, there still is the matter of a proper stroke. Then, as if this weren't enough, there is the task of reading the green to determine the amount of grain in the grass and how it will affect the speed and direction of the putt. But don't despair. These things can be learned, and the knowledge is at your fingertips on the following pages.

Knowing Grass Can Help

To play golf is to play on a golf course, and a golf course is composed mainly of one thing—grass. On the course, at least, Carl Sandburg's famous line is appropriate: "I am the grass; I cover all." If the rough is deep, it may keep its promise and cover your ball.

Grass is the basic surface on which the game of golf is played. In this sense, it corresponds to the hardwood court in basketball, the soft green felt in billiards, or the smooth concrete slab in shuffleboard. Although grass is a fundamental condition of golf, there are as many kinds of grass as there are materials used to build tennis courts. And just as one type of tennis court will "play" differently from another, types of grass vary, too, and differ in their effect on a golfer's game. Even a beginning tennis player immediately notices the difference between a concrete and clay court, but the average golfer may have trouble defining the more subtle varieties of grass used on golf courses.

There are two basic types of grass used on golf courses: Bermuda and bent. There are almost infinite varieties of these two, but these are the fundamental strains. The easiest way to tell the two apart is to remember that bent grass does exactly what its name implies—it bends. Bent grass is allowed to grow longer than Bermuda, and the tops of the leaves curl over and lie flat, so that the length of the blade is bent almost double. Bermuda grass, on the other hand, looks like a crew cut. It is much shorter than bent, and it is bristly and stubby to touch. The two grasses have very different kinds of characteristics.

Bermuda grass is used mainly in the South and Southwest because it stands up well under hot, dry conditions. Bermuda is generally more grainy than bent, and the grain it does have is usually more consistent. The grain on some Bermuda greens is produced almost entirely by the cutting pattern of a lawnmower. Bermuda grass is thick, and its large, coarse leaf makes for a slow putting green. Bermuda greens have less break, too, because the heavy leaves keep the ball from sliding off. The grain on a Bermuda green, however, can radically affect the break or speed of a putt. Going with the grain, a 10-foot putt is equal to a 6-footer, and putting across the grain can double the amount of break, pulling a straight 10-footer a full 2 feet off line. Because Bermuda greens tend to be slow and bumpy, try to contact the ball at the bottom of your putting stroke in order to get the ball rolling smoothly. Also, make allowances for the grain. If you are putting with it, play the ball toward the center of your stance to avoid getting overspin, and reverse this procedure when going against the grain. Through the green, there are several things to keep in mind. Bermuda greens are closely cropped and are usually hard. You may have to land the ball in front of them and let it roll on. Because Bermuda is thick and full, it makes excellent fairways that yield perfect lies. But for the same reason, it becomes an impenetrable rough when left to grow. In tangled, matted grass, don't try for distance. Take what you need to get back to the fairway, and play it safe. Bermuda rough grabs the clubhead, and you may leave the ball right where you found it.

Bent grass is found mainly in the North, although a few Southern courses (Augusta National and Pinehurst) use it. It is a cool-weather grass, and its fine leaf makes for a smooth, true and slick putting surface. Bent grass can be very grainy, especially near mountains and water, and a good hint to remember is that the grain on such courses will grow *toward* the mountains and *away* from the water. Because bent greens are so fast, play the ball more toward the center of your stance as you would on a straight downhill putt. Bent fairways are not as easy to hit off of as Bermuda. Because the grass is thin and soft, and the turf soft, too, there is a tendency for the player to hit every shot fat. And on some bent fairways, especially in the Midwest, patches of clover creep into the bent, producing flier lies. Confronted with his ball lying in clover, the player should take one club less, and try to pick the ball clean.

Even great players are sometimes confused by kinds of grasses. When Bobby Jones was only 14, he went up from Atlanta to the hallowed Merion Cricket Club to play in his first Amateur Championship. One hole at Merion was a relatively short par-three, with a green that sloped toward the tee and a stream that guarded the front of the putting surface. In a practice round, young Bobby played a fine iron shot to a point on the green above the hole. After looking over his putt, he took the center-shafted putter that he used in those days and rapped the ball smartly at the pin. He watched horrified as the ball took off on the shining bent green, rolled straight past the hole, over the green and into the water. Right then, he learned the difference between Bermuda and bent.

Be Ready to Putt

by Chuck Malchaski

You can make a contribution to golf and increase your enjoyment of the game by helping to speed up play. And you can do this simply by being more systematic in your putting routine. Why not try these things the next time you play? (1) When you are 20 yards from the green, start studying the line between your ball and the cup. You get a lot better view of the slopes and contours from the front or side of the green than you do when you're on it. (2) Carry your putter up to the green. Don't wait until you are on the green to pull it out of the bag or take it from the caddie. It not only saves time, but with the club in your hand you subconsciously start to get a feel for the putt. (3) Your first impression of a break is the best one. When you overstudy a lie you become confused and indecisive. Then try not to think about how hard you should tap the ball. Let your instinct take care of this. (4) Get your grip before you step up to the ball. Don't stand over it, gripping and re-gripping, or you may get so nervous you can't take the blade back. (5) Putt out at every opportunity unless in doing so you violate a rule of courtesy. You may be chagrined at missing the first putt, but you still have the line of the putt and the feel of the putter fresh in mind.

Round Hole Squared Away

by Charles Teal

Most golfers miss an inordinate number of short putts from 10 feet and less, when these are the really makeable ones. First, consider the dimensions of the golf hole and golf ball; (A) the diameter of the hole is 4.25 inches and the diameter of the ball is 1.68 inches. Actually, only half the ball on either side of the cup is enough to tip the center of gravity and cause the ball to drop. Now (B), you have lengthened the diameter of the hole to 5.93 inches or by half a ball on both sides. Second, since it is far easier to putt at a cube or square than it is at a circular object, replace the round hole concept with a four-sided one. If you can reach the hole you can make it four ways: in the left or right-hand side, the back, or the front. You can only miss if you leave it short. In practice, then, take a cardboard (C) and cut out a square 2.57 inches on a side, or a full ball-diameter less than the diameter of the hole. *If your ball touches any portion of this cardboard square you have made the putt.* Using this guide will raise your confidence, lower your score and, in actual play, you'll have the psychological advantage of seeing the hole look like a basket.

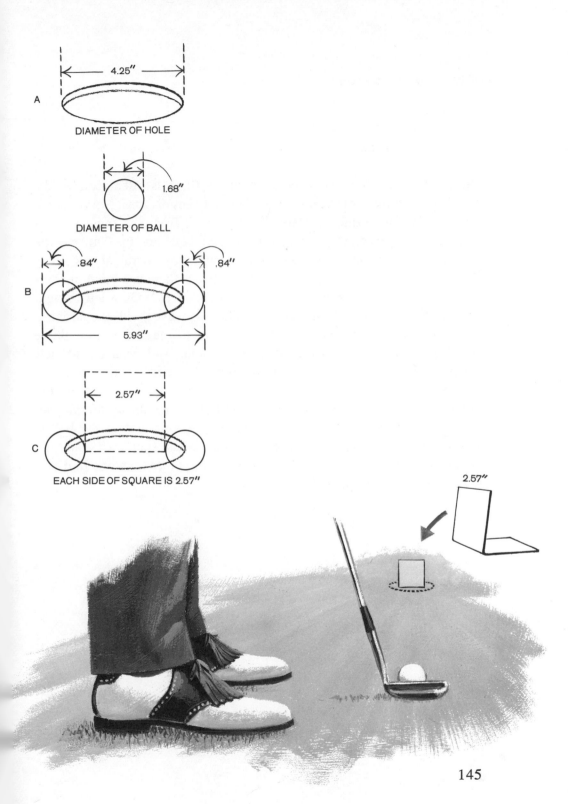

A

4.25"

DIAMETER OF HOLE

1.68"

DIAMETER OF BALL

B

.84" .84"

5.93"

C

2.57"

EACH SIDE OF SQUARE IS 2.57"

2.57"

145

Give Yourself a Break

by Jim MacLaughlin

Playing the ball from the same position on all putts often requires the twisting and turning of the clubhead. This way lies disaster. Not all putts, however, are the same, nor are they to be hit from the same relative point in the stance. Depending on the putt at hand, the ball can be positioned in any one of three different ways. For a straight putt, play the ball on the inside of the left heel. If, however, there is a break in your line, then the ball position should be properly altered. On a left-to-right break, play the ball off the left toe. This maneuver will encourage a strong stroking action that will hold the ball to the left and eliminate pushing off straight or to the right of the hole. And on a right-to-left break, position the ball off the right foot. This ball position prevents premature pulling of the ball to the left and promotes a firm putt on the break line. In addition, two other "musts" to be remembered are playing the ball as close to the feet as possible and making certain the ball is stroked on the middle of the blade—the "sweet spot." If you take advantage of the breaks, you will probably drop more than one putt you would normally have missed.

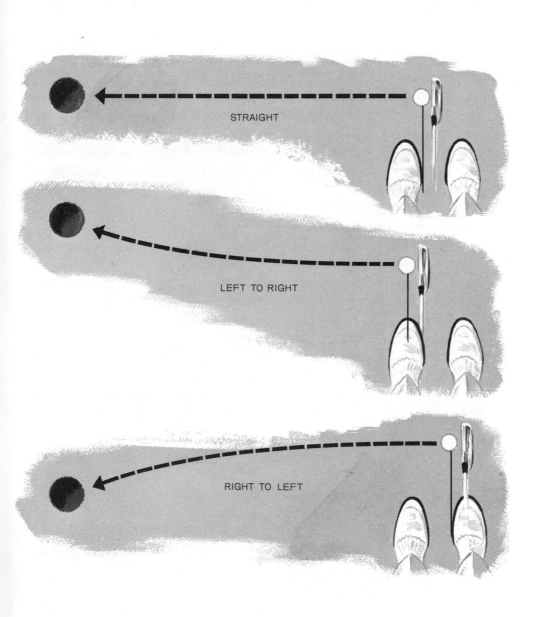

STRAIGHT

LEFT TO RIGHT

RIGHT TO LEFT

One-Putt Prescription

by Harry Pezzullo

The records prove that the difference between winners and losers, even on the professional tour, is the ability to make those three- to seven-foot putts. Why are they missed? After years of observation, the reason seems to me to be, primarily, body movement. To correct this movement and to control the body is not as difficult as it might at first seem to be. First, spread your feet farther apart than at present. Second, point your left knee inward slightly and keep your weight on the inside of the left foot with the ball played about four inches inside the left heel. Once you are set, stay put. Don't fidget around. Third, on the putt itself, use an arm stroke instead of trying to get the body into the shot. You'll find that with your left elbow out you can keep the putter lower (avoiding the quick pickup with a lot of unnecessary wrist action). This low stroke will also keep the putter more easily on line. Locking the body will not only prevent any rocking motion but ensure to a large extent getting down those really makeable one-putts. And if there is any place where you can shave as many as three to six strokes a round, it's on the green.

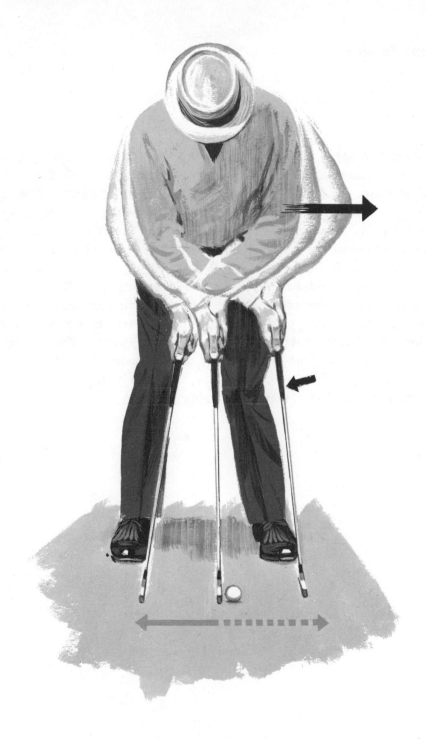

Don't Be Short

by Bill Jelliffe

It seems that nearly all long putts wind up short of the hole, so I have a simple formula which I feel can be of great value to everyone plagued by this problem. It's what I call my "1-foot-for-every-10-feet" system. In other words, if you are 10 feet from the cup, *stroke the ball hard enough to reach 1 foot beyond the cup.* If you are 20 feet from the cup, aim for a spot 2 feet behind the hole, and, from 30 feet, stroke it hard enough to go 3 feet past. If the putt is over 40 feet, I try to envision a washtub around the hole, and merely concentrate on getting the ball inside that imaginary circle. One other important thing: Ordinarily, when you see that your putt is going to slide past the cup, in your disgust you fail to follow the ball from that point on. *Watch it closely until it stops,* because it will tell you how the green breaks coming back. So don't leave it short—and by keeping your eye on the ball until it stops you'll greatly enhance your chances of making it coming back.

15'

1½'

The Casual Conceder and How to Make Him Honest

by Jack Woolgar

At one time or another you probably have met some of golf's perennial pests. They are found in both sexes and on private as well as public courses.

Specifically we refer to the dawdlers who invariably mark their score-cards while still on the green. Or the penny pinchers who hold you up interminably while they search for a beat-up, three-for-a-dollar ball. Forget not those careless citizens who think sand-trap rakes are for groundkeepers' use only—or those characters who chatter while you are addressing the ball.

The list goes on *ad nauseum*. But what really gets a good golfer's goat has nothing to do with the above-mentioned petty problems.

For a real rage-rouser there is nothing quite like the habitual chiseler. Whenever you are afflicted with one of these loathsome liars your blood pressure and score suffer.

These win-at-any-price parasites have a complete bag of tricks. They kick the ball out of the rough, surreptitiously tee up on the fairways, and conveniently have a lapse of memory when it comes to adding up strokes. They play winter rules all summer and no rules all year.

However, our nomination for chief goat-getter is not to be found among the accepted hazards or the canny connivers. The pain-in-the-neck we have in mind is scrupulously honest with his score, plays the ball where it lies, and is a perfect gentleman or lady, as the case may be.

Golfers, we give you the Casual Conceder!

For the benefit of those fortunate enough to be unacquainted with this individual, the casual conceder operates on the theory that any putt less than four feet is automatically in the cup.

Now this works out fine, if it is your putt that he concedes. It isn't. See what happens if you attempt to pick up your own one-footer!

His system is simple. Try for a one-putter. If it doesn't drop, pick up for two. There are never, but never, any three- or four-putts on his card.

152

At this point you are no doubt wondering why this picker-upper is allowed to get away with it. Surely, you think, it should be a simple matter to yell, "Hey, that isn't a gimmee! Putt it out."

This none too subtle suggestion does not work. We tried it. The C.C. merely placed the ball a foot or so closer to the pin, glared at us and snapped, "Fussy, aren't you? I thought this was a friendly game."

There was no use hinting that he had moved the ball nearer to the cup. There weren't any marks on the green to prove it. Then this otherwise honest character calmly proceeded to sink the abbreviated putt. His "Well, I hope you're satisfied" sneer left us feeling furious and futile. Some days you can't win.

Then again, maybe you can—provided the following foursome is sufficiently far behind. Our proposed equalizer goes like this:

Measure all his self-conceded putts and note them on the back of your scorecard. He may growl, "What's the big idea? You trying to be funny?"

Shrug it off with the remark, "Just checking, pal. Just checking. May want to pick up myself, sometime."

If this method doesn't work, you still have another gimmick left. At the end of the game, ask if he would bet on dropping a 40-foot putt consistently. Being essentially honest, the C.C. probably will admit that he'd be satisfied to make it in two putts. Now you've got him!

"Fine," you say, producing your scorecard. "My figures show that you conceded yourself a total of 44 feet in putting. I'll just add two more strokes to your score."

This should do it. But if the C.C. persists in his unorthodox habit, mark him off as a bad risk. Or else concede the whole game before you start.

How's that? Suppose you are paired with a lady casual conceder? Close your eyes, pal. A true golfer is a gentleman at all times.

VII. TROUBLE SHOTS AND CHRONIC AILMENTS

It seems contradictory, but it sometimes is the case that the better you get, the more trouble you get into. After spending much time and effort getting rid of the slice that plagues all beginners, the golfer who has reached a certain level of competence then finds himself battling hooks, shanks and other ailments that generally afflict only relatively good golfers. The purpose of this chapter is twofold. The first aim is to help the golfer avoid or cure such things as the hook and shank. The second is to show him how to get out of the trouble that these misdirected shots have left him in. Obviously, the part about trouble applies to everyone, because no one gets into more difficulty than the duffer with his big slice. Here, then, is something for everyone, including tips on playing in bad weather and on courses that are in less than ideal condition. Read the information carefully and apply it wisely.

The Anatomy of the Hook

The hook is the tragic flaw of the great. Many of the game's outstanding players had to fight it at one time or another during their careers. Most beginning golfers, on the other hand, are slicers, inclined to cut across the ball from the outside—a swing that produces a clockwise spin on the ball and causes it to go far off line and lose distance. For these players, the hook may be only an occasional peccadillo.

But if the average newcomer to the game is an inveterate slicer, his more elite counterpart, the hooker, is usually just as deep in trouble. Whereas the slice bends to the right and is the result of an outside-in swing, the hook curves to the left and is the product of the exaggerated inside-out stroke. The hooking ball rotates with a counterclockwise spin, and it rolls forever after it hits. If the ball stays in the fairway, this roll is an advantage. If it lands in the rough, it is not.

Although neither is desirable, it is probably better for the novice to be a hooker than a slicer—at least it indicates potential and a promise of better things to come. The hook is the result of strong hand action, and if not overemphasized or misused, strong hand action is the key to good golf. Great players usually come naturally equipped with strong hand action, and so they also come naturally equipped with a hook, which they work to overcome. Hogan, Nelson, Jones and Palmer were all hookers, but none became winners until they had learned to hit the ball straight (even with a slight fade) and keep the ball in play. When Hogan first turned professional, he hooked the ball so badly that observers predicted he would never last on the tour. He would play beautifully for stretches of holes, but it seemed there was always a point in every round when a disastrous quick, smothered hook would put him in such difficulty that his score would be ruined.

The most common cause of the hook is a faulty grip. The pros have come to call the hook grip the "strong grip," and it is the one most normally assumed by the beginning player, probably because it is like the

The chronic hooker brings the clubhead into the ball along a pronounced inside-out path that produces a counterclockwise spin. The bottom drawing shows the correct path—straight.

156

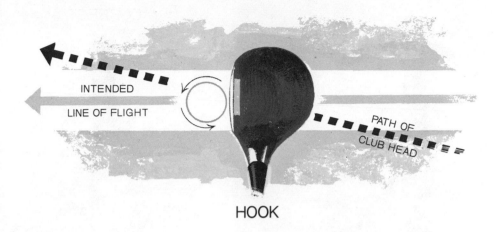

INTENDED

LINE OF FLIGHT

PATH OF
CLUB HEAD

HOOK

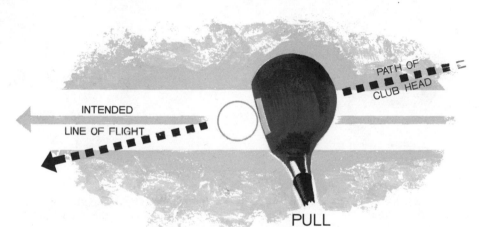

PATH OF
CLUB HEAD

INTENDED

LINE OF FLIGHT

PULL

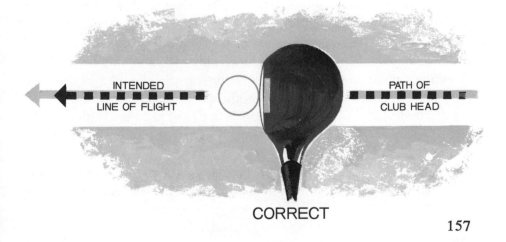

INTENDED
LINE OF FLIGHT

PATH OF
CLUB HEAD

CORRECT

157

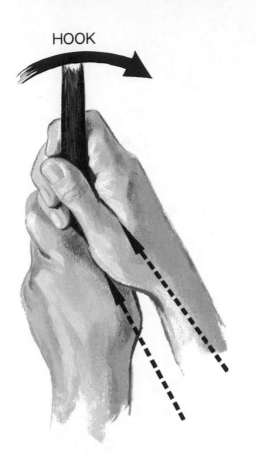

HOOK

CORRECT

Left: the hook grip. The V's point to the right hip; three knuckles of the left hand are visible. *Right:* the correct grip. The hands are not under the club; the V's point to the right shoulder.

grip used to hold a baseball bat. The club is held in the palms of the hands, with both hands turned too far to the right so that the V's formed by the thumbs and forefingers of each hand point outside the area of the body and somewhere in the vicinity of the right hip. The chronic hooker usually can see three or more knuckles of his left hand, and he probably grips the club very tightly. With this sort of grip, the clubface on the backswing is closed and points up in the air. On the normal downswing, the clubhead is brought into the ball in a closed position, with the face turned to the left. The result: a sweeping hook that is likely to run out of control.

In the early 1940's, Jimmy Demaret, a persistent hooker, began experimenting with a new grip. Demaret moved his left hand over to the left until his thumb was directly down the shaft and he could see only one half to one knuckle of his left hand. He then placed his right hand on the club so that the V formed by the thumb and forefinger pointed at the chin. By weakening his grip, Demaret corrected his tendency to overpower the ball with his right hand and, in doing so, cured his hook.

Ben Hogan adopted his friend Demaret's grip, refined it and made it popular. But this "weak grip" is probably not the grip for the beginning golfer—even the beginning golfer who hooks. Congenitally a left-hander (he changed to right-hand golf because of the inavailability of left-handed equipment), Hogan was equally strong in both hands. His left hand was so developed that it could prevent the right from taking command, even when weakened by turning it to the left. The average player's hands are not this strong. Even if he is a hooker, he should take as normal a grip as possible, with the V's aimed at the right shoulder and the club in the fingers rather than the palms. However, if he continues to hook with the hands in this position, he should adopt the Hogan grip.

In taking his stance at the ball, the hooker should check to see whether he is unconsciously hooding the clubface as he addresses the ball. He may be lining up correctly but toeing the blade in as he makes his waggle. This mistake is a sign that his grip is too "strong," and that the clubface will be closing at impact—with a hook the inevitable upshot.

A hooker instinctively aims to the right to allow for the bend. He closes his stance, moving his right foot back from the line of the stance, and aiming his hips and shoulders to the right of where he wants the ball to go. This compensatory adjustment only compounds the error. It is better to address the ball with feet, hips and shoulders parallel to the intended line of flight.

Standing too far from the ball or playing it too far forward in the stance may also lead to a hook. The golfer who has to reach for the ball is liable to swing on a pronounced inside-out arc, and the flattened plane of the swing magnifies the hooking action. If the ball is played forward of the left heel or instep, the player will have a hard time delaying the release of his hands until impact, and he will probably be in the process of rolling them over by the time he arrives at the ball. This rolling is a certain hook-producer.

It is best to use as upright a swing as is comfortable for you, especially if you are prone to hook. It is interesting that both Hogan and Palmer,

159

Aiming to the right to compensate for a hook compounds the error—it accentuates the inside-out arc. Address the ball with feet, hips and shoulders parallel to the line of flight.

pronounced hookers in their salad days, are very flat swingers, and the slightest tendency to get even more flat (say on a big tee shot) may bring out a recurrence of the hook. Jones, who had a more upright swing, began his swing by drawing the club almost directly inside so that it almost touched his right hip. He was then forced to loop it back to the correct hitting line, but any flaw in timing ended up in a hook.

The basic cause of the hook is the dominating right hand, and all the adjustments of grip, stance and swing are designed to make the two hands work together with neither overpowering the other. Tommy Armour and Jones always felt that they were holding on with the left hand and "hitting like hell" with the right—and this is the way it should be. The critical instant where the right hand is most likely to take over is at the top of the backswing just before starting down. The left hand must not be allowed to weaken or lose its firm grip on the club. If it does, the right hand will take charge and precipitate a premature uncocking of the wrists, the "hitting from the top" that is one cause of the hook.

Two other faults may produce a hook. (1) A right elbow that is not kept close to the body during the swing may cause the player to allow the right hand to dominate the swing. The two factors work together and are almost inseparable, so tucking the elbow in to the side will help to make the hands work together—and vice versa. (2) Rotating the shoulders on a horizontal rather than a vertical axis often results in the right shoulder being higher than the left at impact. A smothered, pulled or snap-hooked shot is almost a certainty.

Because he shares the weakness of professionals, the beginning player who is prone to hook his shots may be smug simply because he is not a slicer. But the hook can destroy scores as suddenly and surely as any slice. Don't be proud of your hook. Get rid of it.

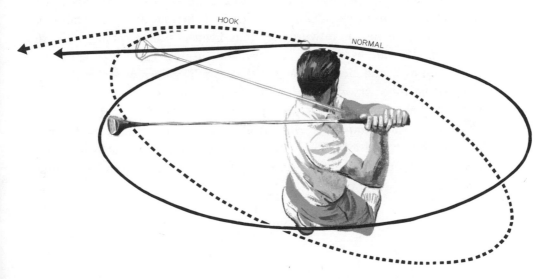

The dotted line traces the flattened arc that produces a hook. A clubhead traveling along this arc will come into the ball on an inside-out path as in the first drawing. Try to use as upright a swing as you can and you will come into the ball straighter.

Cure the Smothered Hook

by Homer R. Reese, Jr.

How many times have you hit the ball solidly or driven through the hitting zone with what you felt was good contact and yet the ball reacted strangely? Instead of performing like a solid hit should have, it probably flew out low, left and then left even more in a nose-diving duck hook. The fact of the matter is you have hit the ball flush—but the face of the club was hooded at impact. The direct cause of such a distance-robbing ailment is *an improper shoulder turn*. By bringing the right shoulder across the chin on the downswing, your head is pulled off the ball. In addition, the club is thrown out low and around the body while the hands roll over and close the face of the club. The correct movement for eliminating those smothered shots is simple. First, *keep your head still* over the ball. Second, keep your body behind the shot with the *right shoulder moving under the chin*. And third, strive for a more upright follow-through and a higher arc by *driving the left shoulder into a high position*. These three checks should give you solid hitting with solid results.

Two Clubs in One

by Ed Golen

All of us have found our ball in the rough or woods nestled up against a rock or tree, in such a spot that it's impossible to hit it with your normal swing. Didn't you ever get the idea you would like to carry a left-handed club to pull off those trouble shots you can't get at right-handed? But to get this extra club poses two problems. First, investing in a left-handed four- or five-iron, which probably wouldn't be used more than a few times a season, and, second, which club to leave out in order to keep within the 14-club limit. But the answer is simple. *Get a blade putter with an angle back and a steel shaft.* If the angle is near 23 degrees, it will be about like a four-iron. The steel shaft will allow you to get more distance from the club. It's legal, and many companies make such putters. The back doesn't need any grooves to do the job, as a sand-blasted surface is just as effective. And with a little practice, you can at least get good enough with this club to save a few penalty strokes. *This gives you two clubs in one*—and it really works.

BACK OF
PUTTER LOFT

APPROX. 23°

Recovery Is the Key

by Don Siok

Recovering from a poor shot is something we all have the ability to do, but seldom go about with the proper attitude. Most high-handicap players, and many lower ones too, become so infuriated with a dubbed shot that they *lose their concentration for the next stroke*. Statistics showing the performance of the top touring pros would amaze you, because the greens hit in regulation per tournament average no more than 13 a round. And yet scores indicate better. This leaves five or more holes where the player must play a pitch, chip or bunker shot. These, in my opinion, are the shots that make or break a good round of golf. How many times do you find yourself hitting a poor shot and then automatically "giving up" on the hole? Remember, golf is a fair game as well as a tough one. It's fair in the respect that it offers more than one chance to make par. If you miss a green and chip closely for a one-putt, you've saved strokes. *Determination and concentration will make you think a better game.*

Stay in Position

by Cliff Cook

A shot from a downhill lie is tough for anybody, and especially so for the average weekend golfer. There certainly isn't any one tip that will ensure a good shot every time, but there are a few things to remember that will help. First of all, play the ball back in the middle of the stance. Second, and probably most important, *you have to stay in position,* so you don't move down the hill and past the ball. Because of the downhill slant, the weight is almost entirely on the left side, and you can't shift normally with a full hip turn on the backswing. If you then try to move your body normally on the downswing, you'll move past the ball every time. The result will be a topped or bladed shot. Downhill shots should be hit *mostly with the arms and hands, with a minimum of body movement.* The third point is simple. A ball hit from a downhill lie will normally move left to right, so compensate for this. The downhill shot is a tough one to master, but swing easy, keep the body still and the results may surprise you.

USUAL HIP TURN

Get Rid of That Shank

by Lew Worsham

One of the most feared and ugly shots in golf is the shank. And once you've got them, watch out! I've seen many golfers who are plagued by the shanks actually shudder when they pick up the wedge or nine-iron—and thinking and fearing the shank only seems to make it happen more often. The only way to cure it is to realize why it happens and then adjust the swing. Essentially, in order to shank, the club has to come into the ball from outside the line you're swinging on. To prove this to yourself, take any wooden board (or even your golf bag) and lay it down parallel to your intended line of flight. Place the ball an inch or so away from the board. If there is any action of pushing at the ball with the right side, you will hit the board before you make it to the ball. If you hit the ball without touching the board, you haven't shanked. Practice it. If you stay back off your toes, keep the body still and don't lunge forward trying to meet the ball in the center of the club, you should start making good contact. The shank is just about the most discouraging shot in golf, but it really isn't that hard to shake.

Slope Strategy

by Sonny Ryan

Success on uphill-downhill shots requires a little more swing strategy than usual. In general, maintaining balance is the key factor throughout the swing—and achieved most easily by *not swinging hard*. The idea is to keep the shoulders as near normal as possible and the hips, especially, remaining level. Shooting *uphill,* the *left knee* should be flexed more than on a flat lie and the ball should be played more toward the *left foot*. Since the uphill tendency is to pull or hook the ball, compensate by aiming a bit to the right of the target. And lastly, choose a less-lofted club to counteract the higher trajectory of the uphill angle, which will decrease distance. Most golfers consider the *downhill shot* the more difficult, although it's only the uphill situation in reverse. Here the right knee should be more flexed and the ball positioned more toward the *right foot*. Aim a little more to the left of target since the tendency downhill is to slice. And again, since the down-slope angle hoods the blade more, this shot calls for a more-lofted club. Both shots can be partially reduced to at least these two rules: (1) Flex the knee that's highest on the slope. (2) Play the ball off the foot that's highest on the hill.

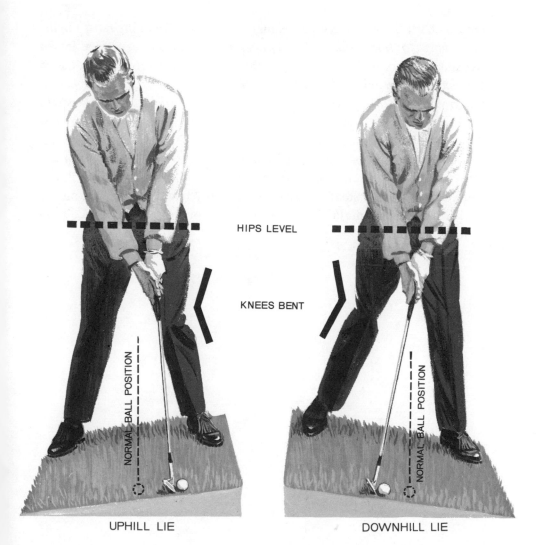

HIPS LEVEL

KNEES BENT

NORMAL BALL POSITION

NORMAL BALL POSITION

UPHILL LIE

DOWNHILL LIE

Balance Is the Key

by Bob Reith, Jr.

On a sidehill lie, where the ball is higher than your feet, *the most impor-tant thing to think about is balance.* Poor balance causes a lot of weekend golfers to fall away from this shot even before they come in contact with the ball. *When taking your stance, plant your feet firmly on the ground. Then flex your knees slightly so as not to have the weight back on the heels.* This will put you in a strong position to maintain your balance. Grip down lower on the club, play the ball back in your stance, that is, more towards your right foot. *Aim your shot to the right of the target as there is a tendency to hook the ball from this lie.* Now if you can keep your head steady to help prevent any lateral movement on the backswing, and maintain your balance, you should be able to make solid contact with the ball.

Golfer's Enemy No. 1—The Shank

Shanking is like any vice—it is hard to stop once you start. The shanked shot is so inimical to good play that Paul Runyan ranks it as the most destructive fault of all, worse than a slice or hook because it costs the player distance *and* accuracy. The really disquieting thing about that first shank is its terrible proclivity to lead to another shank, and then another, until even a solid player is so unnerved that he can produce nothing but a demoralizing series of laterals that careen sickeningly off the hosel of his club. Seized by a spell of shanking, the golfer's muscle-memory fails him. His mind goes blank. He has no recollection of what a correct swing feels like. He expects the very next shot to be a shank. And unless he understands the cause and cure of the fault, it probably will be.

When a player shanks a shot, he has struck the ball with the hosel of the club, the rounded joint that connects the shaft to the clubhead. Usually in the incorrect swing pattern of the shank, this juncture becomes the leading "edge" as the club sweeps into the contact area, with the clubface lagging calamitously behind. The result is a shot that whirls off directly to the right, at a 90-degree angle to the intended line of flight. There is also one other effect: fear.

Professional golfers and teachers consistently emphasize the importance of the grip and stance to beginners. Because of the almost ritual tendency of teachers and instruction articles to monotonously intone this idea, most players ignore it as jejune or stale advice. But the great players know that when they hit a bad shot, it is the result of something they did *before they ever began the swing*. The correct grip and stance is more than a mere prelude to the swing itself. Like an overture, it is functional and organic to the swing as a whole, setting the stage (to continue the metaphor) and aligning the parts of the body for what is to come. Good golf begins with a good grip and a good stance. Apodictic advice, but especially true when dealing with the shank.

The first step, then, in correcting the shank must be to adjust the golfer's grip. Tour performers commonly use the "weak" grip, made popular by Ben Hogan as a ready solution for chronic hookers. The V

This drawing, which looks like a road map for Junction City, shows that a shank can result from almost any kind of swing: outside-in, inside-out, or even straight-through.

formed by the right thumb and forefinger points to the chin rather than the right shoulder, and only one or two knuckles of the left hand are visible to the player as he takes his stance. This grip is not for the beginner, and certainly not for the beginner who has a propensity to shank. The hands of professional golfers are strong and muscular from day-in, day-out play. The tyro's hands are not as powerful, and the "weak" grip may tend to block the normal and desired release of the hands in the impact zone and possibly prevent him from ever getting the clubface into the ball. With his hands turned so far to the left and on top of the club, the novice has trouble sweeping the face of the club squarely into the ball. The club stays open, the face lags behind the hands and never gets into the hitting action at all. The shank of the club does the work instead—and it does a thoroughly bad job.

The correction is simple. Place the hands so that the V's formed by both thumbs and forefingers point to the right shoulder, grip the club surely rather than rigidly, and keep the wrists lissome.

More shanks are the result of an improper stance than any other error in the swing itself. The chronic shanker is very tense as he makes his address. He stands much too far from the ball, and thus his weight is predominately on his toes. His knees are stiff and locked. His arms are tense from overextending and reaching. He is precisely aligned for another shank.

Standing too far from the ball forces him to yank the club directly inside so that it almost brushes against his right hip. At this point in the swing, he then reroutes the arc of his swing, picking his hands up suddenly and sharply, to avoid entanglement with his own right hip. Already deep in trouble, he flattens the plane of the swing further to compensate for this brusque movement with his hands—he "lays off" the clubface at the top of the backswing so that it is parallel with the sky. Poised

When a player stands too far from the ball at address, he puts himself in an awkward position—almost as if he were on a sidehill lie. His weight is on his toes, his body is leaning out of position, and he is rigid. The result, *right,* is that the player's body has pitched even farther forward during the swing itself, and he has rocked into such a position that the clubhead is beyond the ball and cannot hit it.

awkwardly, rigid from the strain of the unnaturalness of the swing his faulty stance has lured him into, the player lurches downward, rocking the upper portion of his body forward. At this crucial point in the swing, the shanker makes either of two moves: He accentuates the already flat plane of his swing, slanting obliquely into the ball from the inside and leading with the hosel of the club; or, in an effort to realign his plane in mid-swing, he forces his hands and arms outside so that the clubface, as it enters the impact zone, is actually *beyond* the ball, and only the shank of the club can make contact.

If you realize how difficult it is to swing correctly when you are on a sidehill lie and the ball is below your feet, how you must struggle to assume a perfect stance to avoid shanking, you should also see how the stance of the chronic shanker precipitates his faulty swing. When you are on level ground, why create an address problem that is peculiar only to a sidehill lie? When the player stands too far from the ball with his weight on his toes and his body inflexible and rigid, he has produced for himself a sidehill-lie type of difficulty. Inevitably, his body will pitch forward during the swing. Inevitably his swing will be too flat. And inevitably he will shank.

Keep the weight on your heels as you stand up to swing. Not all of it need be there if that is uncomfortable—a bare preponderance if that is what feels best. As for relation to the ball, Byron Nelson, for one, says that you *cannot stand too close to it* (unless, of course, you step on it), but if you begin to feel crowded, move back enough to be relaxed. The key to the stance is comfort and naturalness. Any strained, awkward or tense posture will produce a strained, awkward, tense swing.

Keeping loose and easy, take the club straight back from the ball, rotating the shoulders on a vertical rather than horizontal axis. Then return the club to the ball along the same slot as the backswing and hit through the ball. At no time should you flip or jerk the clubhead along the plane of the swing, for such motions tend to promote freezing or locking at the critical instant of contact. Freezing in the hitting area will cause a shank because as the arms and hands stiffen, the clubhead trails irretrievably behind, and only the joint of the club reaches the ball.

Above all, if you begin to shank, do not panic. The insidious nature of the shank steals into a player's swing, undermines his confidence and makes his mind go blank with fear. The best cure for the shank is: *STOP AND THINK*. Do not rush to the next shot, for you may subconsciously attempt a makeshift compensation. For example, many golfers in the throes of shanking, automatically make their swings more flat, thinking this is the cure. Of course, this adjustment compounds the original error. Instead, assume a correct stance, banish tenseness, think only positively, and the next shank you see should be on a steer.

VIII. PRACTICE

There probably isn't a golfer alive who hasn't at one time or another wondered just what was the secret of success of the Hogans, Palmers and Caspers. Well, there is a secret all right, but it probably isn't what you think. The answer lies in practice and plenty of it. There isn't a man on the pro tour who hasn't spent hours upon hours in lonely practice—and every one of them still goes to the practice tee before his round and sometimes afterward. However, just practicing isn't enough in itself; the golfer must know what and how to practice. You can go to the driving range every night for a month, but if you aren't working on something specific all you'll have to show for it will be blisters—and the same old slice. On the following pages are pointers on how to practice and what things to work on. All you have to do then is put them into practice—and practice.

Start Off Like a Tiger

by Bill Strausbaugh

Golf is not as difficult a game to play as the people who play it make it. Everyone who takes up the game, who understands the concept of the golf swing through professional advice, who exercises and practices with some regularity, and who enjoys the challenge of golf, should be able to score between 76 and 85. And all women golfers should be able to score between 95 and 100. This is not exaggeration. Generally speaking, golfers have it in them to play much better than they do without drastically improving their swings or their standards of swinging the ball down the fairway. But in all probability, new rounds will suffer the new golf ball with precisely the same anatomical bruises as the year before. However, such a fate is unnecessary and will become mere legend if you plan ahead.

Just as the earliest subjects taught in school form the basis for all other future learning, so, too, there is a similar process for the golfer. As a preface to understanding the golf swing, it is important to have as few and simple words as possible. Once the basic concepts are in the mind, the golf muscles can then act on them. And it is this muscular response that turns golf into the great sport that it is. But the basic lessons are probably those the average golfer has neglected to take in the first place. These basic mental skills can be learned in a short time, perhaps even in a single session, but the motor skill, the muscular development and response, may take a lifetime.

Actually, any golfer can be taught all he needs to know about the swing in 45 minutes and yet spend the next 45 years teaching the muscles to respond and develop. The average golfer forgets that it takes 12 to 18 months to learn how to walk and instead, unreasonably, expects to swing a golf club correctly in about six minutes.

I admit there is an end to learning about the swing, but there is no end to the application through the muscles of what you've learned. And, if the golfer knows the basics he should still have a check-up lesson before starting the new season and at least four other times during the year. Not that the golfer didn't learn anything on the practice or teaching tee, or that he had a poor instructor, but it is the golfer's only opportunity to have his muscular improvements gauged and the instructor's chance to see whether what was once learned has been forgotten, causing the golfer to fall back into bad habits. Check-up lessons are also a means of putting Humpty-Dumpty, as it were, together again, since the golf course is like the wall he falls off. By omitting such lessons the golfer is really cheating not only himself, but also his professional, who is just as proud to see a player improve as the player is himself. I have found, though, that most golfers are not much better two to ten years later than they were when they started, because they lack what I call follow-up or coaching lessons.

Unfortunately, most golfers haven't even gotten as far as the base lessons. Usually, it's because they feel that swinging a club is the most natural thing in the world and that the advice of a friend or some brief article or other will automatically make them a winner. Nothing is farther from the truth.

The proper golf swing is not a natural but a cultivated art. The unnatural elements are achieving a smooth pivot motion from a stand-still position, the concept of target projection, which holds your optic eye on the ball and your mind's eye on the target area, and the inherent weakness of the left side for the naturally right-handed golfer. It is for these reasons that the golfer needs not only instruction and practice, but also exercises that are swing-related in order to strengthen the muscles and improve the timing. The hands can be strengthened by using a grip squeezer or compressing a handball. Various isometric exercises are excellent winter conditioners. Still, the spring swing is bound to be somewhat anemic. However, if you haven't done a thing physically during the winter then you must play by memory since you have only memory to go on.

Although there is no real need to experiment or tinker with getting a whole new spring form, you should at least have your grip re-examined and swing checked out.

The basic grip should be taken with the left thumb at the two o'clock position. The back three fingers of the left hand should squeeze the shaft. Then the right hand should be placed palm first and snug against the shaft with the pressure applied with the fingers of both hands. A good test of your grip is to consider the club as a hammer and pretend you are driving in a spike. If in your test your hands feel as if they would hammer with strength then your grip is both firm and correct.

As far as the swing itself is concerned, the golfer should alert his mind to the fact that there are not fourteen swings, or one for each club. *There are two and only two*. The first is the *pivot* or *distance swing;* the second is the *pendulum swing*—used from inside 50 yards.

The pivot swing has just three reference points: *target, stretch* and *spring*. Target is really a shortened form of the words *target projection* and, in itself, is a simple concept. It is based on the fact that we really have two eyes, the optic (or seeing) eye and the mind's (or retention) eye. The mind's eye retains a picture of the distance to the target. The same two eyes are used in fielding and throwing a baseball, kicking a field goal, playing basketball and shooting pool. These latter sports are not involved in great distance whereas golf is the only sport in which you speak about distances in terms of hundreds of yards instead of inches or feet or a few yards at best.

Consider the following brief examples of target projection. In basketball, the dribbler may know from the familiarity of the floor where he is in relation to the basket. This perception remains in his mind's eye, but when he jumps to shoot, his mind's eye (or target projection) and his seeing (or optic) eye—which actually sees that target and measures the distance—suddenly join or merge. In shooting pool the player lines up behind the ball and sights over and behind the ball. He may look up many times to fix in his mind the actual distance and precise direction he wants the ball to go. In the stroke itself, his optic eye rests only on the back of the ball as he strikes it with the cue stick. As a matter of fact, this is quite similar to the putting stroke, in which target projection is so much easier than in hitting long irons or woods. A third example of target projection is found in driving an automobile. With his optic eye a man sees the close distance directly in front of him, and with his mind's eye he sees or pictures the greater distance down the road he has to travel.

In golf, now, the mind's eye is focused on the target area down the fairway while the optic eye is fixed on the ball. In the good golf swing the two eyes are not divorced but merge. And here is where *stretch* and *spring* come into play. On the backswing the golfer *stretches* with the upper part of his body away from the target until his back faces the target area. From the top of his backswing, he then *springs* with the

184

lower part of his body in the forward swing (*not the downswing*) and turns his stomach toward the target.

Both the weight shift and the golfer's ability to swing straight through the ball are determined by this understanding of target projection. The mind must be focused on the fairway, retaining a picture of where you want the ball to go.

One method of learning how to swing—not hit—the ball down the fairway is to attach the ball mentally to the clubface and try to fling it down the fairway. You can even cut off half a plastic practice ball and tape it to the clubface. You will actually "feel" the difference in your swing and in your attitude toward the swing. It will soon be self-evident that *you can't make the proper swing and hit the ball at the same time!* The two are incompatible. Instead, let the ball get in the way of the swing.

In a way, golf is a game of destiny, the destiny of the golf ball, which resides in the golfer. The ultimate destiny of the golf ball is some spot down the fairway or on the green. This involves necessarily the idea of target projection and therefore it is not so much the golfer's swing that must change as it is the swinger's concept of the object of his swing. *The worse the swing, the more you must work on target projection.*

The second of the two swings is the *pendulum*—to be used for distances under 50 yards. The reference points for this swing are *triangle, track* and *target*. The triangle refers to the figure formed by the hands, arms and shoulder line when the club is gripped. It is really an upside-down triangle. The pendulum swing, then, is the proper move made by this *triangle* along an imaginary straight *track* to the *target*.

To regain that lost "touch" around the green, one method is to toss a ball underhanded up to the hole. This action performed rhythmically will soon permeate into the swing itself. Then approximate the same rhythm and strength of the toss by swinging the club along the track as though the ball were attached to the clubface. In general, after any layoff, the pivot swing will be faster to recover than the pendulum swing.

Three of the greatest problems brought to the new golf season are not really mechanical but mental. The first is *fear*. The golfer is afraid of missing the ball and as a result becomes too conscious of the ball sitting there. Mentally, some days you can see only the pin and on others you observe only the ball, hazards and penalties. To see the first means your mind's eye is on target; to see only the second means your mental confi-

A good method for regaining the "touch" of the pendulum swing around the greens is shown here. Once you've practiced by throwing the ball underhanded to the pin, the feeling for accuracy should then quickly penetrate into the swing itself. Since the chip shot is being directed not at a large green but at a hole only

dence has collapsed and you've probably left your real swing on the practice tee or in the clubhouse. The second mental defection is *lack of retention*. What happens is that the basic ideas of the pivot swing (target, stretch, spring) and the pendulum swing (triangle, track, target) have vanished in the long winter silence and the golfer has reverted to bad form. He is now overtly trying *to hit* the ball instead of *swinging it out there* and letting the ball get in the way of the clubhead. The third and last mental lapse is that what has been given to the golfer in simple form has spawned an appendix with an anchored head, heel lift, open stance here and a forward press, bent knees and a waggle there. These additions only lead to unwanted confusion, an inhibited swing, and the subversion of what was once well learned.

As for strategy tips, the average golfer should practice getting down in two from off the green since he is more often short than not. He should learn to judge his distances correctly with each club and choose the right club rather than press the shot. When there is trouble on the left or right of the hole, he should tee up on the side of the trouble and *play away from it* instead of at it. And lastly, he should analyze the round he's just

186

a few inches wide, it is vital to align yourself carefully before making the shot. Placing an umbrella or a similar object along the line of flight during practice will enable you to line up correctly.

finished playing. He should ask himself how many times he took three to get down from off the green and how many times he holed "gobblers" or "snaked" one in from a distance. The first tells you how many strokes you gave to the course and the second tells you how many you stole back. And if you compare what you steal with what you give and find that you've given more than you've stolen then you know where your game is weak and exactly what you must practice.

Regarding practice, it is a truism that golfers are lazy as sin. It's impossible to sharpen your game if you don't practice. If Arnold Palmer, for example, went to Alaska you can bet he'd take a net along with him. And yet, the average golfer doesn't come near practicing enough or, if he does, he doesn't do it sensibly. To begin with, you cannot practice any more than 45 minutes intelligently. Second, you should keep a set number of balls—35 to 50—in a shag bag and hit those out three times. That should be more than enough. And third, you should concentrate on the reference points of your swing when you do practice. You should remember that you have two sets of muscles working in the swing: the big muscles in the pivot for distance, and the small muscles in the pendulum for accuracy and control. If you have good distance quality in your practice sessions but you have no control, then your pivot muscles are in good working order but your small muscles in the arms and hands are at fault. To correct this, practice with the wedge and work up to the five-iron. If you are weak on distance but strong on control, then work with the five-iron and on up to the driver.

Whenever it is you start the new season, the right order of importance is to begin with a clear mind and your muscles in shape. If you add to that the proper instruction, swing-related exercises and drills to develop strength and rhythm, and at least 45 minutes on the practice tee, you will spring into the new year with sudden scoring success.

Put the Squeeze on Par

by Alice Kirby

One of the greatest pleasures in golf is giving the ball a long ride. Women are no different in this respect. Women today want to whack the ball a ton. If they hit it 150 yards, they want 200 and so on. Sooner or later, all my pupils ask, "How can I add distance?" It's true women are weaker than men physically, but they *can* compensate. One great help to strengthen hands and forearms is a simple little exercise that takes from five to ten minutes daily. *Try twisting a towel—a plain bath towel. Hold the towel with one hand and twist toward your body with the other. Twist as tight as you can. Repeat the exercise with the other hand.* One of the biggest faults that costs high-scoring golfers distance *is cocking the wrists too quickly on the backswing. This mistake goes right back to weak hands and wrists.* Once you strengthen your wrists, it will be much easier to sweep the club straight back away from the ball.

Don't Cramp the Stick

by Marcel Desjardins

You cannot get maximum power out of your swing unless you have perfect weight distribution and balance. I have noticed after returning to my summer or winter club that during my absence a number of players would have begun to sway either to the right or left while swinging without realizing it. There had to be some way in which they could easily check themselves. *So I cut a hip-length section of broomhandle and put a nail in the end. Do this and then, after taking your stance, place the stick in the ground an inch or two to the side of your right foot so that it runs up perpendicular to your right side—the same distance in your stance from your shoe as it is from your hip.* Now forget about the stick and make your backswing. *Check at this point. If you are cramping the stick, you are swaying to the right. If you have pulled away from the stick, your weight is too much on the left side. If at the top of your backswing, the distance between the stick and your right side is the same as when you started your swing, then your weight distribution and balance are perfect and you should be getting your maximum power.*

Correcting a Grip Fault

by Jim Windsor

You can't play consistent golf with a faulty grip, and the best way to check on your grip is at hand right in your own home—namely the closest wall. *In the perfect grip, the arm, wrist and open palm of the left side should be in a perfectly straight line. So simply put your left arm, wrist and the back of the hand flat against the wall, lay the grip of the club across the palm and simply close the fingers without moving the wrist or the palm of the hand. Then all that's left is to put the thumb straight down the top of the shaft.* It is amazing the number of people who are in trouble right from the start by arching the left wrist or turning it too far over. The wrong start puts the pressure on the thumb and forefingers—instead of on the last three fingers of the left hand where it should be. *Your right-hand grip will be correct if your left hand, wrist and palm are straight as they take their grip. The right hand forms a channel with the two middle fingers and permits the shaft to lay in between them, and those two fingers form the right-hand pressure.* So put your arm, wrist and the back of your palm down along a wall, merely close the fingers of the left hand, and you'll discover that your grip troubles are over.

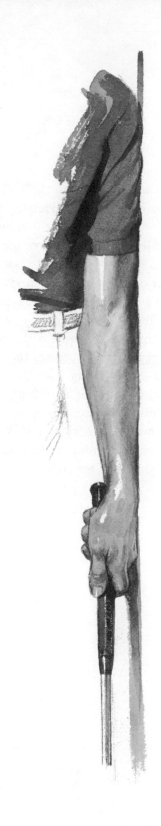

Hitting Through the Ball

by Art Vogt

To hit the ball solidly you must hit through the ball. However, the expression "hitting through the ball" is not understood by many players. To accomplish this a number of things in your golf swing must be right. The head must be over the ball in the hitting area, the shoulders and hips must function properly and a weight shift must take place. It is impossible for a golfer to remember or focus on all of this; it is only possible to think of one thing during the golf swing. The best method or technique I have found to help these fall into place is the image of driving a wedge of wood under a door. To do this stand beside a doorway with the door open. Place your left foot against the doorcase, then in slow motion—without actually using a golf club—swing back and into the ball. This exercise will give you the feel of the weight shifting to the left side and the left hip moving against and away from the wall, as should happen in the properly executed golf swing. The right shoulder will then automatically move down and under while the left shoulder, instead of swaying to the wall, will be higher than the right.

Practice in Reverse

by Marty Lyons

The value of indoor practice can never be overestimated and it's something you can do easily, grooving your swing and setting your grip solidly, by using the club in reverse. One of the destructive mental hazards of swinging indoors is the feeling that the clubhead will strike the ceiling. You can overcome this and get the job done at the same time by *reversing the club so that the grip is toward the floor. Take your grip on the thin bottom edge of the shaft just above the hosel with the toe of the club facing the floor.* Now, of course, you are swinging a very light weight and you will be pleasantly surprised at *how suddenly you are conscious of all parts of the swing with the accent on how you are taking the club back, and whether you are getting full hand action as you go through the "ball."* You will discover that the benefits of working the club "in reverse" are manifold.

Home-style Improvement

by Jack Isaacs

"Feel" is the total answer in golf, and while interminable practice is the only answer to obtaining it, you don't have to go near a golf course in the process. *You can do it with a padded wall in your garage, one of those fiber doormats and the rug in your living room.* I am, personally, proof of my contention. I hadn't accomplished anything of note in golf until I was almost 42 years old. *I spent one whole winter hitting a few hundred balls a day off a mat in my garage, learning to control the ball with my hands. Other times, I spent hour after hour putting on the living-room rug and developed a fine touch that the fastest green could never hinder.* It paid off, because I won the Virginia Open the first time at 42 and the last of five times at 52. I reached the semifinals of the PGA Championship at 45 and qualified for the British Open after I was 50. So I repeat: You can improve your game without going near the golf course. All it takes is desire and that do-it-yourself "home kit" which is so easy to acquire and use.

Practice the Follow-through

by John J. Gavins

Most golfers who slice have poor right-hand and right-arm action at impact. They attempt to aim or steer the ball rather than hit through. As illustrated in the *incorrect* position, the slice is caused by the arms being widely separated coming through the ball. The follow-through doesn't go much farther than shown here because the right hand and arm are blocked. To hit the ball squarely and with power you need a fluid follow-through. In the *correct* position, the right arm turns over just after impact and the club continues to go straight through to the desirable high finish. Keep in mind that I emphasize *right-arm position*. It is vital. If you are a wild and chronic slicer, it is easier to concentrate on getting that right hand to come through than trying to think of your hands working as a unit. In fact, my advice is to forget your left hand and let your right hand do the work in the downswing—at least until you have cured that slice. Then, you won't want to change.

CORRECT

INCORRECT

Practice Length and Line

by Tony Kowski

Like most club professionals, I became interested in golf through caddying. It was during my caddy days that I learned a most valuable putting tip, one that I still use in my instruction format today. Accuracy and distance are the two most important elements in putting. The simplest method to achieve these two is to take about 10 to 12 balls onto the putting green and start by knocking the first ball in the hole from no farther away than 1 foot. After sinking that 1-footer, place the second ball about 6 inches farther back and knock that one in. Keep moving the remaining balls back about 6 inches at a time and don't leave a spot until you knock that putt in. By the time you get 8 to 10 feet from the hole, you probably won't be making the putt on the first try, but you should be certain that you are hitting the ball with enough force to get it past the hole if it does not go in the cup. This will teach you distance. Then concentrate your entire efforts on taking that putter blade straight back and straight through the ball and you will soon have the necessary distance and accuracy to become a good putter.

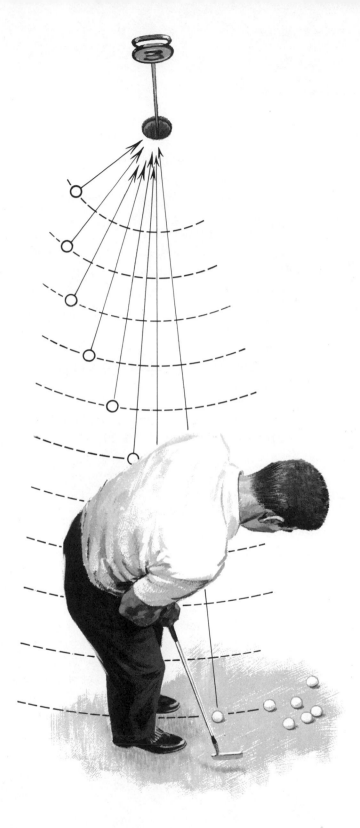

Judging Distance

Tommy Armour had a point. Put the ninety-shooter, he said, in the same spots on the fairway as Hogan, Snead or any other professional, and the master will beat that ninety-shooter by ten strokes—and just because he knows which club to use.

Judging distance is a crucial part of golf. Few things are more discouraging than seeing a perfectly struck shot fall short of the green or carry over on the fly as a result of choosing the wrong club. The ability to gauge distance demands a certain amount of the innate skill of depth perception, but the tyro can improve his judgment by using a few techniques.

Practice is essential. It is the quickest way to arrive at a knowledge of one's potential, the surest way to achieve familiarity with the range of each club. Practice also develops a repeating swing so that the beginner can start to hit his shots the same length every time; he won't be crushing the nine-iron 180 yards one time, and patting it 90 the next.

Ben Hogan was probably the first golfer to make a science out of the art of judging distance. Hogan (and lately Jack Nicklaus with his cartographic, precision-notated scorecards) perambulated about the course during practice rounds, amassing and mentally charting significant facts. So when Nicklaus says he is 156 yards from the pin, he *knows*. Using physical landmarks as guides, he has paced off and recorded all significant distances between points.

This surveyor's technique is fine for golfers who play most of their games on a very few courses, but there will always be times when he is face-to-face with a layout he has never seen. Or he may be in a place on his home grounds where he never expected to be. In this case, Gary Player and other pros use the progression system of estimating distance. The player picks an object (a tree or a bush) that is wedge distance from the ball. Such smaller distances are easier to assess. He then moves his gaze forward 10 yards and rests it on another landmark, calculating that he will need one more club for each additional 10 yards beyond the original marking point. By a series of such mental steps, he can visually work his way to the green—and choose the right club.

If somehow you cannot get a good perspective on the green, pick out something around the green such as a tree, and by focusing on that, estimate the distance from your ball to the putting surface. Greens are flat and lie horizontally with the land so they are often hard to distinguish from the rest of the fairway. A tree stands out against the sky, and its vertical silhouette is a better marking point. Also, if there is a sand trap in front of the green, it may be more simple to visualize what club you would need to land the ball in that trap, and then take one more so you can clear it.

If there are no hazards to affect your decision, and you are struggling to decide between one of two clubs, remember that most greens are three clubs deep—that is, you can hit one club to the front, one to the middle and one to the back edge. There are two schools of thought on whether to choose the greater or the lesser club in a borderline situation. You should select the lesser club, one group maintains, so you will go ahead and hit hard and not try to baby the extra club and end up quitting on the shot. But other teachers say the opposite: use that extra club so you won't have to force your swing. Practice can tell you which error you are more likely to fall into.

In desperation, the lazy golfer can always ask what his playing partner is using to reach the green, and then select his own club on that basis. This is a dangerous habit, and one which the old professionals continually exploited. Walter Hagen was a master at the ploy of loudly calling for too much club, and then watching as his hapless opponent would follow suit and fly his own ball completely over the green. Tommy Armour told a story on himself. Playing with young Horton Smith in a tournament in Oklahoma City during the late 1920's, Armour decided to try a little gamesmanship. At a short par-three hole, he openly asked his caddy for a club that was at least three clubs too strong for the distance. But by cutting the shot, he managed to manipulate it onto the green. Armour was hoping, by his gambit of the finessed shot, that he could trick the young Smith into relying on Armour's judgment instead of his own. But Smith ignored Armour's choice of clubs. He took a club much less than the one the Silver Scot had used, hit the ball into the hole for a hole-in-one, and won the tournament.

He knew the importance of judging distance.

IX. THE PROPER EQUIPMENT

Major league baseball players use bats that are the correct weight, shape and length to produce optimum results. Good bowlers have a ball that is drilled precisely to fit the size and shape of their hand. The same is true of all good athletes, including top golfers. Why, then, does the duffer persist in buying a random set of clubs "off the rack" when the odds are tremendous that they won't suit his build or ability? In case you didn't know it—or chose to ignore it—your game will improve appreciably if you get clubs that fit. On the following pages is information not only about the proper clubs, but on care of equipment, what clubs you should carry in the bag, whether or not to wear a glove, etc. You'll find that the game is much easier if you use the proper equipment and take care of it.

What Every Golfer Should Know About Clubs

by Peggy Kirk Bell

Golf clubs are being built with amazing precision. It is now possible to fit accurately any golfer who tees it up. Golfers have become very particular about having the right club for their height, weight, build and strength, whether they shoot 70 or 170. And, although I feel that many players put too much emphasis on swing weight and gross weight, etc., it would benefit the beginners if they became a bit more informed about the golf club, how it's constructed and why.

In fitting clubs, I take into consideration two basic elements—the physical characteristics of the golfer and his particular stage of development. For the pure beginner, I suggest a set of three-, five-, seven- and nine-irons, sand wedge and putter in the irons, and driver, three- and four-wood in the woods. In fact, the average beginner is better teeing-off with the three-wood because of the added loft on this club. It will give him confidence and also enable him to get the ball airborne. This set gives the golfer a chance to learn to hit a few basic clubs and is more practical as far as the pocketbook is concerned.

I think, however, our primary concern is with the golfer who is starting to get it around pretty well and now wants to buy a full set of clubs. What interests him the most is very simple: "What particular clubs should I have in my bag and what kind fit me best?"

It's very difficult to fit a person with a set of clubs without some knowledge about how the golfer strikes the ball. I think it's very unwise of golf pros to attempt to suggest clubs merely on the basis of how big or little the player is. I'm constantly amazed at the petite girls who come along and can pump the ball out there pretty good. And the hefty ones who swing at the ball as if it were made of glass. I always have my members hit a few shots to get an idea of what they are capable of doing.

Also, the pro should have confidence in how the club feels to the golfer. There have been times when I have suggested such and such a shaft to a player only to have the golfer go to another shaft because it *feels* better. In the final analysis, it is the expert guidance of the golf pro plus the ability of the individual to determine the club that feels best.

There are some general rules of thumb that you can be guided by. The major manufacturers build standard golf clubs with three types of shafts: stiff, regular and flexible. The swinging weight, which means how the club is balanced according to clubhead, shaft and grip, is designated with the symbols C-2, C-5, C-7, etc.; the heavier the shaft and clubhead, the heavier the swing weight.

If, for example, a golfer hits a club hard to the point where he'll be pulling the ball or fighting a hook, I try giving him a stiffer shaft and little heavier swing weight. If on the other hand he has been playing with a pretty stiff shaft and has trouble either getting the ball up in the air or is hitting the ball way to the right of the line, I will advise a little softer shaft and less weight in the clubhead.

Other considerations are the size grip a golfer should have, and, in some instances, the length of the club if the golfer is particularly tall or short. As for the grip, the pro can tell just by looking if it is all right. If a golfer has unusually small hands or short fingers, a thinner grip can be ordered without too much trouble.

Other questions that keep popping up are: "What woods do I need in my set now, should I have a four-wood, five-wood, or what?" These are questions that can only be answered for each particular case. I know that women want the pitching wedge in their bag as soon as possible because they have to depend on their short game more than a man does. Also, they hit the woods more often than they hit the two-iron, and I personally think this is a good idea. Women golfers normally need to hit two wood shots to reach average par-four holes. Therefore, the four- and five-wood get as much if not more use than any other club in the bag. Depending on the manufacturer, the four- and five-wood usually have more loft on them than the two-iron, giving the gals a chance to get the ball in the air—which in the first few years of play is of primary concern to all beginners.

The last tip I would like to pass on is about the use of the sand wedge. I find that golfers develop an early aversion to sand traps. They either try to pick the ball out with a seven- or eight-iron or timidly cut it out of the bunker. I know I get my golfers to use the sand wedge right from the start. I make them go after the ball in the trap. This eventually develops a positive approach to a bunker and also the other shots in the bag. The sand wedge is a good club to practice with because of the weight in the head of the club. It helps strengthen the hands early in the player's development and it contributes to building good hand action. Your golf clubs are very personal things. A little thought about them will result in lower scoring and more enjoyable rounds.

Take Care of Your Equipment

Your golf equipment usually amounts to a sizable investment and, therefore, it's only common sense that you should try to keep it in good condition. By simply spending a few minutes after finishing a round of golf, you can maintain that like-new quality.

SHOES—Be sure to clean the dirt and grass from the spikes and soles before you place your shoes in the locker or car trunk. Keep them polished and treated with a good leather conditioner and use shoe trees to keep the shoes in shape. Check periodically for loose or missing spikes.

BAG—You will be wise to initially select a bag of ample size. A bag too small can cause damage to grips and shafts. If you have a leather bag, treat it at least twice a year to keep it from cracking. Whatever type of material your bag is made of, you will be wise to spend a minute wiping off any dirt or dust that usually accumulates during a round of golf. Whenever there is evidence of wear in the strap, replace it to avoid the inconvenience of having it break while you are on the golf course.

WOODS—No set of woods can be expected to last too long if the golfer neglects using head covers. These covers protect the woods from nicks and scratches that can appear if they are left unprotected to bang against the irons. An occasional coat of furniture polish that also contains ingredients to remove stains and ball marks will help you keep your woods in their original gleaming lustre. Always use a soft cloth, however.

IRONS—No one can expect to play their best golf with irons that are clogged with dirt. You can keep your irons clean by simply soaking them in warm water for a short period. Then clean out the grooves with a scrub brush, but never use wire or steel brushes as they tend to scratch the faces.

GRIPS—You can keep your grips clean by wiping them with a damp cloth that has been soaking in lukewarm water containing a mild detergent. Your golf professional can recommend several products which will help you restore original tackiness to leather grips.

Such periodic personal care will help you keep your fine equipment looking as good as new. If you have any major repairs, however, such as broken or bent shafts, or loose grips, etc., don't try to do the work yourself. Stop in and see your professional who has the knowledge to make these repairs. If he can't do the job, he will certainly recommend someone who can. In the long run, you'll probably find out that it's cheaper this way, too.

Taking everything into consideration, the equipment you purchase in your professional's shop may cost you a few dollars more, but remember, you are getting the finest equipment available and you are assured of playing with clubs that personally fit *you*. Admittedly, thousands of clubs are purchased yearly from discount houses or department stores, but if your game has progressed beyond the beginning stage, you should be playing with clubs that fit. Your professional, knowing your game, is best qualified to pick the clubs that will allow you to play your best golf. When you buy that set, take care of them!

Why a Golf Glove?

Once upon a time, as the fables begin (though it was more likely in the late 1920's), a venerable wealthy Scot was golfing at Gleneagles. He was formidable off the tee, but also egregiously wild, due mainly to his chronic inability to maintain a firm grip on the club. At last, one drive flew over a clump of trees and buried itself deep in the heather, but the gentleman, cut from the archetypal Scottish mold, tramped in after it. He lost sight of his foursome, but kept up the search, all the while musing over the problem of his unsure grip. Suddenly, he came upon, of all things, a young farm lass, sitting placidly in the midst of a clearing and milking her cow. On her left hand, she wore (most strange!) a glove, and in answer to the obvious question, she told the Scot, "It helps my grip." In a heat of inspiration, he purchased it from her on the spot and ran back to show his companions. From that day forth, he was never without the glove, and he played happily ever after. The golf glove was born.

Natives of Gleneagles swear that this apocryphal story is true, and indeed it may be. If so, it is a contemporary of a similar American account of the discovery of the golf glove, a story only slightly more prosaic. H. G. Hilts & Co. were the manufacturers of the first commercial golf glove, and it was probably Harry Hilts who made the original fortuitous discovery. Hilts rarely played golf but was lured into a game one day by a prospective customer. Surprisingly, the threesome also included one E. G. Willard, Hilts' biggest competitor for the guest's business. Hilts, who did not even own a set of clubs, was playing poorly and being baited by both his customer and the leering Willard. Finally, Willard challenged Hilts to a bet, wagering that he could outdrive him on the seventh hole. Wet and cold from a steady drizzle that had been falling since play began, Hilts by now was enraged. He rushed to the next tee and, without stopping to remove the pale gray dress gloves he was wearing, drove ferociously into the mist. It was the longest drive of his life, and he won the bet easily.

The first glove produced by the company was called the "Hilts Golf Palm." Made of thick leather, "the palm" was not really a glove at all: It had no fingers and covered only the center of the hand. In the 1930's, Don Willard (the son of E. G.) designed the short-fingered glove, which was simply a regular man's glove with the fingers cut off. The development then progressed to the open-backed design, and by the mid-1930's, the full-fingered glove as we know it today.

Although Hilts' original conception of the glove had been as an aid to holding onto the club, the early products were similar to work gloves, very heavy and loose-fitting, designed more to protect the hand from blisters than to prevent slipping. But toward the end of the 1930's, the manufacturers began to emphasize feel, and the gloves became softer, thinner and more tight-fitting.

A few players such as Leo Diegel and Lawson Little made extensive use of golf gloves before World War II, but most of the great players (Jones, Hagen, Sarazen, Mac Smith) ignored it. But after the war, the innovation of smaller grips and club handles forced many golfers to use a glove in order to prevent the spindly club from turning in their hands as they made their shots.

And so, in the late 1940's and early 1950's, the concept of the glove came full circle and reverted to Harry Hilts' original *raison d'être*. No longer simply a protective device, gloves were carefully engineered for tight fit, tackiness and better feel—almost like a second skin. The glove became by the early 1960's not only an aid to the hands but a fashion item as well, and new flairs, designs and colors achieved big sales. Manufacturers still emphasized a good fit and feel, and worked constantly to improve the rubbering bordering the seams, drawing the glove in to keep it tight. Today, 90 percent of the touring professionals use the full-fingered glove, and Hilts' accidental discovery has grown to a $12-million industry.

The beginning golfer should realize that the glove must fit very tight to be of maximum value. Try it on by putting all four fingers in before the thumb; this technique prevents stretching. To care for your glove and make it last, pull it out to its original shape after you have finished playing. This stretching restores the softness of the glove as the natural oils of the leather rise to the surface and help to restore pliability. Never roll up a glove, especially one soaked with sweat, and do not squeeze it dry. If you wash it, be careful not to wring it out of shape, and let it dry on a towel.

Today's gloves are expensive, the products of strange and exotic leathers from around the world. There are even areas in Africa where primitive native tribes raise cattle to produce hides for gloves, and though they are totally unaware of golf, they seem to know everything about the makings of a good golf glove—a little like that innocent Scottish girl who may have started it all.

X. GOLF CAN BE FUN

Assuming that you have now digested enough of the fore-going information to lower your handicap significantly, the game should start to be more enjoyable. However, learning to play better is only the first step toward having fun on the course. Here is information on a variety of competitions, plus a description of several popular betting games—if you're inclined to wager on your ability. Last, but not least, we have included a section on a few of golf's rules that are frequently violated. Without meaning to be sticky about it, we would suggest that everyone read the section on the rules carefully. A better knowledge of what you can and cannot do will make the game more enjoyable for you and for your playing partners. Have fun.

Put More Fun in Your Golf

Some of the Tournaments Your Club Can Hold

Virtually all the events held on today's professional tour are at stroke or medal play. But at the club level, there are numerous other types of tournaments that can often make the game more fun. Have you ever played in a Scratch and Scramble event or a String tournament? How about a Blind Partner tournament or a "shotgun" start?

The following list will provide you with a description of some of the tournaments which can be held at your club and chances are you will find a few that may be unfamiliar to you or your events chairman.

Team Events

BEST-BALL TWOSOME—Taking handicaps as they fall on the card, two players play as a team. The lowest score recorded on each hole, with handicap, counts towards the team's best-ball score for the round. Although both players play their own ball, only the lowest score on each hole is counted. The team having the lowest best-ball score wins the event.

BLIND PARTNER—Can be played as an 18-hole stroke play round or as a best-ball twosome. Players tee off with anyone of their choice, but partners are not drawn until the last group has teed off. A player does not know who his partner is until he completes his round. Can be played as the best-ball twosome described above, or on a net basis where the two players' handicaps are subtracted from the gross score and the team with the lowest combined net score wins.

SCRATCH AND SCRAMBLE—On each hole, two-man team scores are added and the total score is divided by two to determine the team's score. It is usually more interesting to pair a high and low handicapped player together. Handicap for each team can be obtained by totaling the handicaps of the team and dividing by two.

BEST-BALL FOURSOME—Same as the best-ball twosome except teams are now composed of four players. The lowest score, with handicap, on each

218

hole counts as the team's score. Can also be played using the best two-ball or best three-ball scores of the foursome where the two low scores and three low scores, respectively, are used in determining the team's total.

MIXED FOURSOMES—Becoming very popular at many clubs as a Sunday afternoon event. Male and female teams, husband and wife or otherwise, alternate shots until the ball is holed.

POINT TOURNAMENT—All four balls in the foursome count. Players use their handicaps and take the strokes as they come on the card. On each hole and on a net basis, four points are awarded for an eagle, three points for a birdie, two for a par and one point for a bogey. Five points, of course, go to the lucky fellow who scores a double eagle. The team with the most points wins the event. This event can also be played as an individual event, the winner being the player with the most total points.

Individual Events

MEDAL SWEEPSTAKES—Players play 18 holes and the winner is the player with the lowest net score. Also, a prize may be given to the player with the lowest gross score to encourage participation of low-handi-cappers.

MATCH VS. PAR—Players, using their handicaps as they fall on the card, play against par. For example, if a player's net score on a hole is 7 and par is 4, the player would be one down to par. The winner of the event is the player who is most "up" on par at the finish of the round.

BLIND BOGEY—A good event when the players may not have established handicaps or when accurate handicap information is not available. Players choose their own handicaps to get their net score somewhere between 70 and 80, or between whatever figures the committee may choose. The committee then draws a number between these figures and the winner is the player whose net score equals this number. If no player's net score equals this drawn number, the committee may draw another number.

NASSAU TOURNAMENT—Similar to the medal sweepstakes except prizes are awarded to the players with the lowest net score for the first nine, the second nine and the total eighteen holes.

FLAG TOURNAMENT—Each player is given a small flag with his name attached. Using his handicap, the player plays until he has used the number of strokes totaling par plus his handicap. For example, if par is 70 and the player's handicap is 20, he would plant his flag at the spot where he completes his 90th stroke. If a player has not used up all his strokes after he has holed out on the eighteenth, he continues to play until his strokes are used and plants his flag at that spot.

BLIND-HOLES TOURNAMENT—Nine holes are selected from the eighteen to be played and contestants do not know which holes were selected until they finish. The player's scores on these selected nine holes are totaled and half this handicap subtracted from this total. The winner is the player with the lowest net score for the selected holes.

STRING TOURNAMENT—Each player is given one foot of string for each stroke of his handicap. At any point on the course, the player may advance his ball to a more favorable position, cutting off that amount of string equal to the distance the ball was moved. For example, if a player has a one-foot putt, he may advance his ball into the cup and cut off a foot of string. Once the string is all used, the player is on his own. The player with the lowest score wins the event.

One type of tournament that has grown extremely popular at private clubs is the "shotgun" tournament. Foursomes are spread out over the entire course with at least one team on each tee. Longer holes can accommodate two teams. This type of event is ideal for a large field when it would be too time consuming to have all contestants start from the first or tenth tees.

At a predetermined time, a shotgun, or other suitable blast which can be heard throughout the course, signals the start of competition. Any of the above events can be used. The advantage of the "shotgun" tournament is that all teams finish at approximately the same time. This makes it suitable for a luncheon, dinner or other social activity to follow the tournament. Prizes or awards can be given at this time.

Why Golfers Bet—and How

Why do people bet at golf? Almost everyone bets on sports events, but the peculiar thing about golf wagers is that the *participants* in the game do most of the betting. This situation is almost unique in sports, for the people who play a game do not as a rule have something staked on the outcome. Sports such as baseball, basketball and football, which are ideal for spectator gambling, do not seem to produce betting by the players themselves. Boxers don't bet on themselves. Tennis players rarely put anything on the line, and if they do, it's usually nothing more than the can of balls. The same man, however, who plays touch football and tennis for nothing feels cheated out of a game if his would-be opponent refuses a dollar Nassau on Saturday. Why is the bet such a necessary part of golf?

The answer seems to lie in the very nature of sport itself and its compelling appeal for our civilization. The essence of all sports is competition—an open struggle, fresh and clean, free of details or pettifoggery. Men thrive on challenge and competition, especially when the competition is clearly stated and clearly met. The attractiveness of sport is its simplicity. As our society becomes more and more complex and cluttered with intricacies, it grows increasingly competitive. Or so we are told. But it appears that this so-called struggle is really a proxy competition, waged by only the few in positions of authority, as if they were epic heroes, going out to do battle as representatives of their individual tribes. The man at the Avis desk in the airport has been told that he is in a war with the young lady behind the Hertz counter, but as an average man, pigeonholed in his segment of a cloistered, corporation-dominated world, he understands only the monotony of the daily grind. Nowhere is the challenge, the glory of his struggle clearly stated. But in sport, ah! in sport it is different. Sport, as Albert Camus said, is life simplified, stripped of all the nonessentials, reduced to the basic ingredients: good, evil, winner, loser, force, violence, grace, energy, exhaustion, courage, necessity, idealism, victory.

All of the basic ingredients of this "life simplified" are contained in the crucial element of competition. Competition is a natural concomitant of most sports, but golf is an exception since, for all practical purposes, it can really be played alone, with only the course and one's best previous score as the opponent. People bet when they play golf to produce the element of competition with a tangible opponent that is inherent in most other sports. Without the wager, two players often feel that they are only randomly involved in any sort of game, and each of them may actually feel that he is playing by himself. The bet is the connecting link between the two golfers. It establishes the competition, creates it so that no longer is the player struggling only with himself, but with a flesh-and-blood rival. Any game that can be played alone generally *requires* a wager to state the competition. Thus, people bet on pool, free-throw shooting and golf, but not on ping-pong, basketball and tennis. Betting on golf also relieves the frustrations of the game, for the player is no longer fighting himself, but a palpable challenger.

And so betting is a paradoxical factor in golf. It is the element that makes golf unique (because it is the participants who are doing the betting), but at the same time, it is the catalyst that makes golf like other sports because it establishes the competition with another player. Remember that we are always referring to casual, weekend golf in this article, and not tournament play.

On a less philosophical level, the high incidence of betting in golf is surely attributable to the game's admirable handicapping system. It is necessary for a good bet that the opponents be roughly equal in ability so that there is some doubt as to the outcome of the contest; golf's handicapping techniques effect such an equality, even between two players of disparate skills.

Ellsworth Vines, who was a champion tennis player before he became a pro golfer, recalled that when he was at his peak in tennis, there were only a handful of players in the whole world who could give him an exciting match, but with golf's handicap method, he could have a close, interesting game with any kind of player.

If you are going to bet at golf, you had better be like a poker player and know the house rules before you start. Most wagers are won or lost on the first tee when the game is made up, so know what you are playing and, above all, know your opponents.

The following is not intended to instruct you how to become a hustler in three easy lessons, rather to acquaint you with some of the more

222

common games. Hustling, an art designed to methodically extract tax-free moneys from the unsuspecting golfer, is frowned upon by the USGA—and rightly so. The rules concerning gambling in golf are to protect the individual and the game itself.

The USGA is primarily concerned with organized gambling and not the small personal wagering that goes on between friends. The desire to compete for a dollar, a golf ball or the lunch is not wrong. It's only when the golfer finds himself looking to make a living at it that he distorts the true meaning of the game.

Here is a brief guide to the types of bets you may encounter. Remember, in all the games mentioned, handicaps are used.

NASSAU—The most common kind of bet. At match play, three points are scored: one for the first nine, one for the second, and one for the eighteen. If a golfer is playing a "one-dollar Nassau," he has three individual one-dollar bets.

BISQUE—A handicap stroke that may be taken on any hole at the player's option. Strictly speaking, a stroke that is given to an opponent must be taken at the hole indicated on the scorecard as being that particular handicap number. Thus, if a player is given "five strokes," he must use those strokes on the holes marked one to five on the card. The handicap numbers are usually circled to differentiate them from the hole numbers. A bisque, on the other hand, may be taken anywhere.

SKINS—A skin is awarded to the winner of each hole provided that he is not tied by another player. If two tie, all tie. A deadlier version of this game (and not one for those who play a steady, unspectacular game) is called cumulative skins. In this little hair-raiser, holes not won by anyone because of ties are accumulated and awarded to the first winner of a hole. Also called "scats" or "syndicates."

GREENIE—This is a shot that ends up closest to the hole on par-threes. Again, the winner collects from the other members of the foursome.

TEAM SKINS—Those loyal partners who do not wish to win greenies and skins from one another, play for team skins. If either member wins a skin, it is awarded to the team and not the individual.

BINGLE-BANGLE-BUNGLE—A fast-paced item with lots of action. Three points on each hole: one for the player who reaches the green first; one for the player nearest to the cup after all are on the green; and one for the player who first holes out. Charlie Coe sometimes plays this one with his friends to even out the game, since obviously a consistently good player loses his advantage over the short hitter and the lucky putter.

BOBS AND BIRDS—Bobs are points scored for closest-to-pin on par-three holes only. Birds are points scored for birdies on any hole; double for eagles.

SCOTCH FOURSOME—Partners may alternate driving, two players play against two, each side playing one ball. After the tee shot, the teams play alternate shots until the ball is holed out. There are two variations played in the United States: *1. Selective drives:* Both partners drive on each hole, then select the ball with which to complete the hole with alternate shots. *2. Pinehurst:* Both partners drive on each hole, play each other's ball for the second stroke, then decide with which ball to complete the hole. The failing of this type of play is that the golfer does not hit all the shots.

LOW BALL AND TOTAL—A four-ball team bet in which the best ball of each team wins one point, and the low total of the partners wins another. This game is a method of getting a good bet out of the situation in which there is one very good player playing with a poor one against two average players.

PRESS OR EXTRA—A new bet on the remaining holes. If someone wants to take a "dollar extra" on the seventeenth tee, he wants to play the last two holes for the dollar.

The best advice on betting is never to wager more than you can comfortably afford to lose, or else you may be putting yourself under unnecessary pressure that will probably hurt your game. Don't rush into an extra bet when you are losing unless you have been playing unusually badly and have suddenly discovered the cure, or you have been hitting the ball well, but have been unlucky.

Peripatetic golfers who do not play regularly at one course, and who get into games with strangers, should be wary of what looks like a sucker bet. There may be a hidden kicker. In the musical *Guys and Dolls,* Sky Masterson tells a story that is a good lesson for anyone who is betting with people he doesn't know. Sky remembers that when he was preparing to leave home and start out on his own, his father treated him to some advice in lieu of a bankroll. "One of these days in your travels," he said, "a guy is going to come to you and show you a nice brand-new deck of cards on which the seal is not yet broken, and this guy is going to offer to bet you that he can make the jack of spades jump out of the deck and squirt cider in your ear. But son, do not bet this man, for as sure as you stand there you are going to wind up with an earful of cider."

So if a guy comes up and offers to bet you that he can drive a golf ball two miles, do not bet this man, because remember that this bet has been won by guys driving balls off mountains and down frozen rivers. And a lot of guys have been left with earfuls of cider.

Rules

As he was preparing his second shot on the eleventh hole of the Worcester Country Club, Bobby Jones suddenly straightened up and stepped away from his ball. Turning to an official, Jones announced that he was calling a penalty shot on himself for having caused the ball to move as he was addressing it. The ball had been lying in deep rough; no one had seen it move, and most of the gallery was of the opinion that if it had moved at all, it had been an independent, imperceptible turn that was no fault of Jones. But Jones said no, and insisted that he had precipitated the ball's motion by soling his club behind it in the tangled, matted grass.

Jones incurred this penalty stroke during the first round of the 1925 U.S. Open. Willie MacFarlane went on to win that championship, defeating Jones in a playoff, and everyone became aware of the awful import of that one penalty which only Jones had seen fit to call. For without that stroke on his card, there would have been no playoff, and Jones would have been champion. But when he was asked about this and other penalty strokes that he had called on himself in tournament play, Jones fairly bristled. "There is absolutely nothing to talk about," he said, "and you are not to write about it. There is only one way to play the game."

Despite what Bobby Jones said, at least 75 percent of all amateur golfers are finding several other ways to play this game—they cheat. Sometimes as imperceptibly as the turn Jones's ball made in the rough, sometimes innocently without knowledge of the rules, and sometimes very deliberately. A few rules seem to be abused more than others, and the beginner should pay some attention to them. Here is a list of six that seem to be the most violated of all.

WINTER RULES—Unless proclaimed by the local officials, there is no such thing as winter rules. Rules 16 and 17 specifically dictate that the ball must be played as it lies, and that improving the lie or stance is prohibited. The player is not necessarily entitled to an unrestricted swing and he may not bend tree limbs to give himself room, except in the

226

natural motion of taking his stance and swinging. The club may be grounded only lightly and may not be pressed into the ground as many players do in the rough in order to make the ball stand up in the grass. Penalty: Stroke play—two strokes; match play—loss of hole.

ASKING ADVICE—A player may ask advice only of his caddie, his partner, or his partner's caddie. He may not ask his opponent what club he just used or how that last putt broke. The penalty is two strokes in medal play; loss of the hole in match play.

HITTING FROM OUTSIDE THE TEE AREA—The "teeing ground" is defined by the rules as a "rectangular area two club lengths in depth, the front and the sides of which are defined by the outside limits of the two markers." If a player tees his ball outside this area, he may be required by his match-play opponent to replay the shot from within the markers. There is no penalty. In medal play, the golfer must replay his tee shot, including any strokes he has already made on the hole, under penalty of disqualification. You may use any club to measure the "two club lengths in depth," even a driver.

CHANGING BALLS—The golfer may not change balls on the green or anywhere else on a hole unless it has become unfit for play in the course of that hole. So if the player begins play with a badly cut ball (as he is liable to do on a water hole), he may not change when he reaches the putting surface as his ball did not become unfit for play during that hole. Mud on the ball does not render it unplayable according to this definition. Penalty: Stroke play—two strokes; match play—loss of hole.

LOST BALL—If the player loses his ball, he may not simply drop a new one near the point where he lost the old ball. He must return to the spot from which the original ball was played, adding a penalty stroke to his score on the hole. So if the golfer loses his tee shot in the trees, he must return to the tee and hit another ball, counting both strokes played and adding a penalty shot.

SPIKE MARKS IN THE LINE OF THE PUTT—They may not be pressed down or repaired, and this is perhaps the most violated rule of golf. Touching the line of the putt is prohibited except to repair ball marks or remove loose impediments. The penalty is loss of the hole or two strokes in match play.

It has been said that the dividing line between a duffer and a golfer is the magic score of 90, and that the huge majority of those that play the game will always be duffers. But Bobby Jones says differently. "Anyone who plays golf regularly and with a wholesome respect for the rules and etiquette of the game is a golfer."

It should be the only way to play the game.

75 76 77 10 9 8 7 6